$\mathscr{B}$IBLICAL

$\mathscr{P}$RAYER & $\mathscr{F}$ASTING

Discovering & Experiencing
The Power of God

*"This kind goeth not out but
by Prayer and Fasting."*
(Matthew 17:21)

By Ronald Louissaint

ACKNOWLEDGEMENTS

It would be impossible to acknowledge the many teachers who have made an impact on my spiritual walk such as, Ronald Smith of Faith Christian University and Dr. Odessa McNiell of Eastern Bible Institute, Bishop David Oyedepo of Faith Tabernacle. I am forever grateful to you—thank you. To Pastor Rod Parsley, a general in this generation, for exemplifying Christ to me. To the late E. M. Bounds, Derek Prince, Smith Wigglesworth, Laurore Morisette, Herman Morriseau, Sister Regina, Kathryn Kuhlman, and the writers of notes and authors of books from whom I have drawn over the years concerning this wonderful subject. In the words of the Apostle Paul, anyone who takes the responsibility of writing must say, "Did the word of God originate with you? Or are you the only people it has reached?" (1 Cor. 14: 36, NIV). One can give full glory to the Lord Jesus Christ, who brings understanding, revelation, and illumination to the church by the ministry of the Holy Spirit, whose ministry it is to take the things of the Lord and make them real to our hearts and lives.

Special thanks to Eric Lunkenheimer, my brother in the Lord; my Mother, Fanilia Millien; Daddy Como; my brothers and sisters; Specially Godfroy Louissaint; my friends and colleagues; Pastor Kenny Maseko; David Addison and family; Samuel ulaba Samura; Pastor Wismy Athouriste, Titus Mulamba, Dr. Paulette McIntosh, Pastor Otto Kowbena, Nicole Bury; Sonia Laborde, Rhoda Donat, Kathrina Love; Mr. Steve Lebrun, Yolene Charles; Marie Charles, thank you for the many hours you spent typing for me. To all my folks; and, most importantly, to all the prayer warriors and those who fast and have kept these principles alive throughout history. Evangelist Jacques Taylor thank you.

God bless you all.

TABLE OF CONTENTS

DEDICATION

To my Lord and Savior Jesus Christ. To Miss Perette Lanthia and my son, Zachary—thank you for all your support. To Marie Jose and Marthe Tranquille, who have vital testimonies giving evidence to what God can do when we humble ourselves to fast and pray. And to my young champions: Jordan, Tom David, Jeff, Mike, Shirley, Betty, Stephanie, Nerlande, Anne, Don Craft De'Sevigney, Schneider, Joe, Joshua, Josue, Nelissah, Samuel, and all of you young people out there—you're the best!

FOREWORD

He stilled raging storms, walked on water, cast out unclean demonic spirits, cleansed lepers, healed paralytics, opened the eyes of the blind, the ears of the deaf, and restored the lives of the dead. Jesus Christ performed these miracles and so many more before *His* resurrection so that men might believe and receive the salvation of the Lord. And *He* left those who believe in *Him* with the promise that they would do even greater works! (John 14:12) What an honor to be chosen to continue to advance the Kingdom of God!

O.K. We have this mind blowing promise – right? And the word of the Lord is "Yeah" and "Amen" – right? So, if *He* promised that we would do greater things than those which *He* did, then we are indeed able – right? So, why don't we? Why are our lives not at their maximum state of well being, and the world is in a state of chaos? We have not been praying and fasting as we should. Beloved, as he told His disciples, the men chosen to walk the closest with *Him,* the men who sat right up under the anointing and leadership of Jesus, this kind can come forth by nothing, but by prayer and fasting (Mark 9:29). These two are among the most vitals tools that we must develop and dedicate ourselves to in order to have an impact on the world and the Kingdom!

Needless to say the enemy also knows this. Therefore, his tactic is to blind the eyes of the called, the chosen and the elect to the principles of fasting and prayer. He knows the power of a praying believer! Beloved, I am sure that you have heard the saying P.U.S.H. *Pray Until Something Happens.* Why should we? Because through prayer and through fasting God indeed changes things. The kingdom of the enemy suffers serious defeats. The power of prayer is very real. Do not under estimate it. Souls are won into the kingdom, broken lives are restored, yokes are destroyed, provision is made and so much more!

And that is the fast that God has chosen for the remnant and the fast that this book encourages you to engage in. The type of fasting and prayer that looses the bands of wickedness, undoes heavy burdens, lets the oppressed go free, and breaks every yoke. With effectual and fervent prayer and a biblically guided fast we can deal bread to the hungry, bring the poor that are cast out into houses, impart healing hands, and most importantly win souls (Isaiah 58:6-7).

If you have picked up this book it is because you understand the need to answer the call of the Lord to move to another dimension of prayer and fasting and ultimately spiritual authority. It is because you are among the remnant and desire to be used mightily by the Lord. If you agree, take out a journal and writing tool and prepare to study. Do not simply read this book and then place it on the shelf. Actively study this testimony along with the corresponding scriptures. Let this text serve as a spring board to propel you to a place where God can use you mightily!

In Christ,
Rhoda Donat

INTRODUCTION

"When I [Moses] went up the mountain to receive the tables of stone, the tables of the covenant which Jehovah made with you, and I abode in the mountain forty days and forty nights, I ate no bread and drank no water, —" (Deut 9:9, Darby).

"And she had been a widow for 84 years. Anna never left the temple courtyard but worshiped day and night by fasting and praying" (Luke 2:37, GW).

Prayer is one of the most important rights God has given His children. The Word of God says, "Call to Me and I will answer you and show you great and mighty things, fenced in and hidden, which you do not know (do not distinguish and recognize, have knowledge of and understand)" (Jer. 33:3, AMP).

Prayer is the breath of the regenerated spirit, so it's very important that we know how to go about it. Jesus said, *"And in that day you will ask Me nothing. Most assuredly, I say to you, whatever you ask the Father in My name He will give you. Until now you have asked nothing in My name. Ask, and you will receive, that your joy may be full"* (John 16:23-24). And the Apostle Paul said, "…giving thanks always for all things to God the Father in the name of our Lord Jesus Christ" (Eph.5: 20). Except we know how to pray in the God-given way, we can be certain we cannot receive from Him.

The Scripture says very simply, *"For everyone who asks receives, and he who seeks finds, and to him who knocks it will be opened"* (Matthew 7:8).

But in its simplicity there is also one truth:
we must ask aright.

Therefore, knowing how to pray is as vital as the need to pray. It is often said that the way to learn how to pray is to pray. However, this is not correct. The way to learn how to pray is to be taught. From the Master's mouth, we learn the mechanics of prayer, "When you pray, say: 'Our Father...' " We must humble ourselves and learn like children.

The purpose of this book is to teach effectual prayer. As I have already stated, there is a place for knowledge in prayer, which nothing can replace. Without knowledge we "ask amiss," and asking amiss is the reason some do not receive. "You ask and do not receive, because you ask amiss, that you may spend it on your pleasures" (James 4:3). God is not obligated to answer a prayer that will cause you to sin. (Emphasis mine). This book will teach you how to pray using the Word of God, and the Word of God is the source of knowledge for effectual prayer.

David said,
"I will worship toward Your holy temple,
And praise Your name
For Your lovingkindness and Your truth;
For You have magnified Your word above all
    Your name" (Ps. 138: 2).

And also "Forever, O Lord,
Your word is settled in heaven" (Ps 119:89).

The prophet Isaiah said it best:
"Put Me in remembrance;
Let us contend together;
State your case, that you may be acquitted"
    (Isa. 43:26).

Put Him in remembrance of what? says the Lord. That is the reason the author of Psalm 119:49 stated these words: "Remember the word to Your servant, Upon which You have caused me to hope."

Whenever you bring the Word to God, you can rest assured He will act on your behalf. For that reason, I strongly urge you to learn the Word of God—the only mechanics for a successful prayer life.

CHAPTER ONE

THE *Place* OF *Prayer*

WHAT IS PRAYER?

Prayer is personal communication with God.

In addition, "Prayer is the Christian's lifeline to God, and through it lives are changed for eternity!" said Reverend E.M. Bounds.

Prayer is communion with God. The Bible talks about different types of prayer. Basically, prayer is asking God to get involved in a given situation on the basis of His Word. As you can see, prayer is not telling God about our problems and needs. No! He knows about our problems and needs. *"Therefore do not be like them. For your Father knows the things you have need of before you ask Him"* (Matt. 6:8). Rather, it is the Word of God concerning our need of returning to Him. "So shall My word be that goes forth from My mouth; It shall not return to Me void, But it shall accomplish what I please, And it shall prosper *in the thing* for which I sent it" (Isa. 55:11).

I want to assure you that the principles outlined in this book will work for you if you faithfully follow them. They have worked for me. God has no favorites; neither has He respect of person. Jesus stated in John 16:23-24: "And when that time comes, you will ask nothing of Me [you will need to ask Me no questions]. I assure you, most solemnly I tell you, that My Father will grant you whatever you ask in My Name [as presenting all that I AM] [Ex 3:14]. Up to this time you have not asked a [single] thing in My Name [as presenting all that I AM]; but now ask *and* keep on asking and you will receive, so that your joy (gladness, delight) may be full *and* complete" (AMP).

Every believer has the noble opportunity of confessing the Word of God. "I have been crucified with Christ; it is no longer I who live, but Christ lives in me; and the *life*, which I now live in the flesh I live by faith in the Son of God, who loved me and gave Himself for me" (Gal 2:20). "So you should consider yourselves dead to sin and able to live for the glory of God through Christ Jesus" (Rom 6:11, NLT). It may be that you have quoted these verses many times and still wondered why there is so little power in your life over sin, the world, and the devil, and why you have not been able to walk in the power that Jesus promised. *"The Truth is, I say to you, he who believes in Me, the works that I do he will do also; and greater works than these he will do, because I go to My Father"* (John 14:12). Are the greater works evident in your life? Do you long for the life of Jesus to be more fully manifested in you, yet the flesh remains uncrucified in many areas of your life? Every Christian has three enemies:

    a. The flesh
    b. The world
    c. The devil

The Lord Jesus Christ conquered all three of these enemies

for you on the cross. To the degree in which you conquer them, will be the degree to which Jesus Christ can live His life through you. Since you must conquer by faith the finished work of Jesus that he suffered for you on the cross in which He gave you perfect victory over the flesh, the world, and the devil; it remains evident, therefore, that what needs to be strengthened and increased is your faith. God has not left you without the means to strengthen your faith. Paul gave the church of Ephesus a final admonishment: "Finally, my brethren, be strong in the Lord and in the power of His might" (Eph. 6:10). Two of the strongest and most effective biblical techniques God has given you to increase your faith are prayer and fasting. If you do not want to enter this battle against the flesh, the world, and the devil, don't bother reading this book. However, if the purpose of your life is to use the biblical principles God has given you to glorify Jesus Christ in your life for the salvation of souls, then continue on.

Fasting is a biblical principle taught by Jesus by both word and example for the purpose of Christian growth. There are areas of victory in your life that will never be realized except through prayer and fasting. *"However, this kind does not go out except by prayer and fasting"* (Matt. 17:21). Jesus does not ask you to fast, He tells you to fast. Jesus did not say if you fast, He said, *"Moreover, when you fast,* do not be like the hypocrites, with a sad countenance. For they disfigure their faces that they may appear to men to be fasting. Assuredly, I say to you, they have their reward" (Matt. 6:16). In one of His sermons Jesus taught three spiritual exercises that are necessary in the disciplined life of every Christian. These three indispensable spiritual principles are:

    a. Giving
    b. Praying
    c. Fasting

The purpose of this book is to show the importance of these three principles in your personal fellowship and obedience to God. Jesus taught that they can be done in the right way or they can be done in the wrong way.

The first spiritual principle is giving. Giving should never be directed by man or to man, as taught in many fellowships today. But biblical giving should be unto the Lord and directed by the Lord Jesus Christ alone. The Apostle Paul said, "I know how eager you are to give. And I have proudly told the Lord's followers in Macedonia that you people in Achaia have been ready for a whole year. Now your desire to give has made them want to give. Each of you must make up your own mind about how much to give. But don't feel sorry that you must give and don't feel that you are forced to give. God loves people who love to give" (2 Cor. 9: 1, 7 CEV).

The second spiritual principle is praying. Praying should never be directed by man or to man, but should be offered to God out of a heart filled with the Holy Spirit. Most Christians know to some extent and have practiced to some measure both giving and praying.

A few Christians even know the extreme importance of praying earnestly in the Holy Spirit for hours every day. The word "earnest" means serious determination. When your heart is fixed on something that is determination. Therefore, as used in reference to prayer, earnestness means heartfelt prayer. It is the heartfelt prayer of the righteous that God reckons with. The Amplified version of James 5:16 reads: "The earnest (heartfelt, continued) prayer of a righteous man makes tremendous power available [dynamic in its working]." This is important. It is God's expressed will for you to praise Him. Giving thanks is God's will for you. Prayer is the only way of getting your voice heard in the throne room of heaven. "For you have need of patience, that, after you have done the will of God, ye might receive the promise" (Heb. 10:36, AKJV).

Understand that the Bible says that having done the will of God, you might receive the promise. The promise is your answer. It is what you are believing God for. It will only come after you have done the will of God, which is giving thanks. Come with praise. Be specific. Ask according to His will. Ask in "…the earnest (heartfelt, continued) prayer of a righteous man that makes tremendous power available [dynamic in its working]." The reason why you must be earnest is that God looks into the heart. Half-hearted prayer, or prayer that has origin only in the mind of the person praying, will have little or no effect. Such prayer amounts to the confession of empty words.

Earnestness in prayer means the "pouring out of soul." In 1 Samuel, Hannah was pouring out her heart to the Lord. When Eli thought she was drunk, she replied, "Sir, please don't think I'm no good! Hannah answered. I'm not drunk, and I haven't been drinking. But I do feel miserable and terribly upset. I've been praying all this time, telling the LORD about my problems."

"Eli replied, You may go home now and stop worrying. I'm sure the God of Israel will answer your prayer."

"Sir, thank you for being so kind to me, Hannah said. Then she left, and after eating something, she felt much better" (1 Sam. 1:15, CEV). Being earnest has nothing to do with physical exertions and postures assumed in prayer. The account of Hannah praying in the temple states, "Now Hannah spoke in her heart; only her lips moved, but her voice was not heard" (1 Sam. 1:13).

Fervency in prayer has to do with the heart alone. Your

heart must be fixed on what you are looking for. Elijah was as human as we are, and yet when he prayed earnestly that no rain would fall, none fell for the next three and a half years! Then he prayed for rain and down it poured. The grass turned green and the crops began to grow again (James 5:17-18). Earnestness was the determining factor, and the aim of the Spirit of God in exhorting us to emulate Elijah is simple: that we might have power in prayer. Come with praise. Ask according to His will. Ask in the name of Jesus. Ask in faith. Be earnest.

BELIEVE YOU HAVE THE ANSWER AND GIVE THANKS!

Jesus said, "For this reason I say to you, All things whatsoever ye pray for and ask, believe that ye receive it, and it shall come to pass for you" (Mark 11:24, Darby).

"And blessed is she that has believed, for there shall be a fulfilment of the things spoken to her from *the* Lord" (Luke 1:45, Darby).

The Scriptures emphasize one important principle regarding effectual prayer. You must believe at the time you pray that God has already granted the thing you desire of Him. Believing is seeing, and this is the exact opposite of what the world is accustomed to—that *seeing is believing*. This is extremely important. If you are waiting for the arrival of the thing desired before believing, you will miss it entirely. "That is what the Scripture means when God told Abraham, 'I have made you the father of many nations.' This happened because Abraham believed in the God who brings the dead back to life and brings into existence that which didn't exist before" (Rom. 4:17, NLT).

Believing precedes the manifestation. Therefore, until you

believe, you are not ready for the answer. It is not enough to be told that all things are possible with God. The devil also believes that and trembles at the "earnest (heartfelt, continued) prayer of a righteous man makes tremendous power available [dynamic in its working]" (James 5:16). The reason why you must be earnest is that God looks into the heart. Half-hearted prayer, or prayer that has root only in the intellect of the person praying, will have little or no effect. Such prayer amounts to the confession of idle words.

The third spiritual principle is fasting. Fasting should never be directed by man, but should be a ministry to God out of a heart full of love and thanksgiving for what He has done for you on the cross. It is because fasting has been almost totally neglected that this book has been written. By including biblical fasting in your life, a spiritual balance of these three principles will be attained and your fellowship with Jesus will be deeply enriched, thereby unleashing His unlimited power in your life.

God does not need your giving. You are the one who needs to give that you may be transformed into the image of the great giver who gave His only begotten Son to die in your place and save your soul from eternal hell that you may live with Him forever in heaven. The Bible says, "For God so loved the world that he gave his one and only Son, that whoever believes in him shall not perish but have eternal life" (John 3:16, NIV). There is no power in giving; the power is in Jesus. Giving is only the obedient cleansing of the channel that Jesus may flow through you as He desires.

If you do not know Jesus as your own personal Lord and Savior, get on your knees right now and tell Him that you cannot save yourself. Ask Jesus to come into your heart, and believe Him for always keeping His Word. *"Look! Here I stand at the door and knock. If you hear me calling and open the door, I will come in, and we will share a meal as friends"* (Rev. 3:20, NLT). Invite Him to come now. Because now is your time! And thank Him for saving your soul.

God does not need prayer. You are the one who needs prayer as a channel of fellowship with Him through your Lord and Savior Jesus Christ. There is no power in prayer; the power is in Jesus. Prayer is merely the contact and preparation.

God does not need fasting. You are the one who needs fasting that your life may be transformed. There is no power in fasting; the power is in Jesus. Fasting is only obedient yielding to God that He may do through you what He could not do otherwise. Just as there is a right and wrong way to pray. So there is a right and a wrong way to give. There is also a right and wrong way to fast. The Master Himself left these instructions.

"And now about prayer. When you pray, don't be like the hypocrites who love to pray publicly on street corners and in the synagogues where everyone can see them. I assure you, that is all the reward they will ever get. But when you pray, go away by yourself, shut the door behind you, and pray to your Father secretly. Then your Father, who knows all secrets, will reward you.

"When you pray, don't babble on and on as people of other religions do. They think their prayers are answered only by repeating their words again and again. Don't be like them, because your Father knows exactly what you need even before you ask him! Pray like this:

"Our Father in heaven, may your name be honored.
May your Kingdom come soon.
May your will be done here on earth, just as it is in
heaven. Give us our food for today, and forgive us our sins, just
as we have forgiven those who have sinned against us.

And don't let us yield to temptation, but deliver us from the evil one.

"If you forgive those who sin against you, your heavenly Father will forgive you. But if you refuse to forgive others, your Father will not forgive your sins.

"And when you fast, don't make it obvious, as the hypocrites do, who try to look pale and disheveled so people will admire them for their fasting. I assure you, that is the only reward they will ever get. But when you fast, comb your hair and wash your face. Then no one will suspect you are fasting, except your Father, who knows what you do in secret. And your Father, who knows all secrets, will reward you" (Matt. 6:5-18, NLT).

Set your house (your life or your ministry) in order! It is for this reason that biblical fasting is emphasized in this book.

The excuses people give today for not fasting remain excuses and God's Word still remains the same to them (Isa. 58). Fasting is a spiritual exercise (like prayer) to cleanse the channel so His life and gifts will flow. You do not ask God if you should pray! When a truth is plainly taught in the Word, it is wrong and dangerous to ask for permission of God to break His Word. God does the commanding and He says when you give, when you pray, when you fast, do it in the right way and the spiritual benefits will follow. (Matt. 6) It is a matter of love and obedience. The people who make excuses for not fasting and praying are the ones who need these disciplines the most. Fasting is not a way out for all; it is an act of obedience to God.

Prayer and fasting are the foundations of life. They are not life to the eyes and ears but to the spirit and soul. In fact, prayer is what makes existence worth experiencing. When prayer is absent, there is no sense or stability or desire; the human being is left void of the vitality of life. In fact, prayer is the engine that keeps the believer's life and ministry moving forward. Prayer is to the church and the believer what water is to the body. To maintain a prayer life is not to give oneself to evil, but rather to enter into the fullness of God, which is the fullness of living. A life without prayer is like a person without a spirit, for it is only through communication with God that the spirit man thrives in a world ruled by flesh and the desires thereof. To restrain the spirit from speaking to God is to erase the divinity of man as the image of God and give oneself to the devourer and death.

E.M. Bounds was a prophet of God that was used mightily concerning this revelation, truth and power of prayer. He has taken the consensus theology, past presumptions and false doctrines of prayer and smashed them into a million pieces with his book entitled The Weapon of Prayer. He has taken the basic biblical truths of prayer and spelled them out in big black letters on a banner in the sky so there would be no mistaking its importance, simplicity, and severity. To read The Weapon of Prayer is to look into the depths of divine revelation and discover that you have been getting it all wrong the entire time, according to God. As I began to find myself near death concerning my prayer life, I also found that there was a hope as simple as receiving a gift to keep me in the will of the Father.

E.M. Bounds begins his book on the importance of prayer, and details the route of communication from man to God and vise versa. He then goes on to write on the current state of prayer and the detrimental effects of a prayerless people. He talks about how it is only through prayer that God has the right to move in the lives of men; the prayerless Christian freely exposes himself to the enemy and consequently binds his deliverance and freedom for the lack of his communication with the Father. He then speaks concerning those men and women who want to be effective in ministry and who want to make a mark in their generation that they must be people of prayer. He finishes his dissertation on prayer as a weapon with modern examples of prayer warriors, including holy men and women of God; such people as Hugh Latimer, Frances Ridley Havergal, Girolamo Savonarola, Bishop Thomas Cranmer, William Carvosso, John Wesley, Jonathan Edwards, John Knox, Bishop Polycarp and Blandina.

This old practiced soldier of Christ, Master Hugh Latimer, who was once the persecutor of Christ became his zealous advocate—noted in Foxe's Book of Christian Martyrs.

Frances Ridley Havergal—
Oh, let me know the power of the resurrection; Oh, let me show Thy risen life in calm and clear reflection; Oh, let me give out of the gifts thou freely gavest; Oh, let me live with life abundantly because thou livest.
—J. Vernon McGee's Thru The Bible,

Girolamo Savonarola—1452-1498
It is said that when Savonarola in the city of Florence went before the great populace and said, "Be free," they applauded him. But when he said to them, "Be pure," they ran him out of town.
But I will hope continually. When I cannot rejoice in what I have, I will look forward to what shall be mine, and will still rejoice. Hope will live on a bare common, and sing on a branch laden down with snow. No date and no place are unsuitable for hope. Hell alone excepted, hope is a dweller in all regions. We may always hope, for we always have grounds for it: we will always hope, for it is a never failing consolation.

And will yet praise thee more and more. He was not slack in thanksgiving; in fact, no man was ever more diligent in it; yet he was not content with all his former praises, but vowed to become more and more a grateful worshipper. When good things are both continual and progressive with us, we are on the right track. We ought to be ministers in doing good, and our motto should be "more and more." While we do not disdain to "rest and be thankful," we cannot settle down into resting in our thankfulness. *"Superior"* cries the eagle, as he mounts towards the sun: higher and yet higher is also our aim, as we soar aloft in duty and devotion. It is our continual hope that we shall be able more and more to magnify the Lord.

J. Vernon McGee's Thru The Bible

Dr. Cranmer was deservedly, and by Dr. Warham's desire, elevated to that eminent station.

In this function, it may be said that he followed closely the charge of Saint Paul. Diligent in duty, he rose at five in the morning, and continued in study and prayer until nine: He ranked high in favor with King Henry, and even had the purity and the interest of the English Church deeply at heart. His mild and forgiving disposition is recorded in the following instance. An ignorant priest, in the country, had called Cranmer an ostler, and spoken very derogatory of his learning. Lord Cromwell receiving information of it, the man was sent to the Fleet, and his case was told to the archbishop by a Mr. Chertsey, a grocer, and a relation of the priest's. His grace, having sent for the offender, reasoned with him, and solicited the priest to question him on any learned subject. This the man, overcome by the bishop's good nature, and knowing his own glaring incapacity, declined, and entreated his forgiveness, which was immediately granted, with a charge to employ his time better when he returned to his parish. Cromwell was much vexed at the lenity displayed, but the bishop was ever more ready to receive injury

than to retaliate in any other manner than by good advice and good offices.
—Foxe's Book of Martyrs

He that findeth his life, He who, for the sake of his temporal interest, abandons his spiritual concerns, shall lose his soul; and he who, in order to avoid martyrdom, abjures the pure religion of Christ, shall lose his soul, and perhaps his life too. He that findeth his life shall lose it, was literally fulfilled in Archbishop Cranmer. He confessed Christ against the devil, and his eldest son, the pope. He was ordered to be burned; to save his life he recanted, and was, notwithstanding, burned. Whatever a man sacrifices to God is never lost, for he finds it again in God. —Adam Clarke's Commentary

William Carvosso, an old-time Methodist class-leader, was one of the best examples which modern times has afforded of what was probably the religious life of Christians in the apostolic age. He was a prayer leader, a class leader, a steward and a trustee, but never aspired to be a preacher. Yet a preacher he was of the very first quality, and a master in the art and science of soul-saving. Here are some of his brief utterances which give us an insight into his religious character. "I want to be more like Jesus." "My soul thirsteth for Thee, O God." "I see nothing will do, O God, but being continually filled with Thy presence and glory."

This was the continual out-cry of his inner soul, and this was the strong inward impulse which moved the outward man. At one time we hear him exclaiming, "Glory to God! This is a morning without a cloud." Cloudless days were native to his sunny religion and his gladsome spirit. Continual prayer and turning all conversation toward Christ in every company and in every home, was the inexorable law he followed, until he was gathered home. On the anniversary of his spiritual birth when he was born again, in great joyousness of spirit he calls it to mind, and breaks forth: "Blessed be Thy name, O God! The last has been the best of the whole. I may say with Bunyan, 'I have got into that land where the sun shines night and day.' I thank Thee, O my God, for this heaven, this element of love and joy, in which my soul now lives."

Here is a sample of Carvosso's spiritual experiences, of which he had many:

"I have sometimes had seasons of remarkable visitation from the presence of the Lord," he says. "I well remember one night when in bed being so filled, so over-powered with the glory of God, that had there been a thousand suns shining at noonday, the brightness of that divine glory would have eclipsed the whole. I was constrained to shout aloud for joy. It was the overwhelming power of saving grace. Now it was that I again received the impress of the seal and the earnest of the Spirit in my heart. Beholding as in a glass the glory of the Lord I was changed into the same image from glory to glory by the Spirit of the Lord. Language fails in giving but a faint description of what I there experienced. I can never forget it in time nor to all eternity.

"Many years before I was sealed by the Spirit in a somewhat similar manner. While walking out one day, I was drawn to turn aside on the public road, and under the canopy of the skies, I was moved to kneel down to pray. I had not long been praying with God before I was so visited from Him that I was overpowered by the divine glory, and I shouted till I could be heard at a distance. It was a weight of glory that I seemed incapable of bearing in the body, and therefore I cried out, perhaps unwisely, Lord, stay Thy hand. In this glorious baptism these words came to my heart with indescribable power: 'I have sealed thee unto the day of redemption.'

"Oh, I long to be filled more with God! Lord, stir me up more in earnest. I want to be more like Jesus. I see that nothing will do but being continually filled with the divine presence and glory. I know all that Thou hast is mine, but I want to feel a close union. Lord, increase my faith."

Such was William Carvosso—a man whose life was impregnated with the spirit of prayer, who lived on his knees, so to speak, and who belonged to that company of praying saints which has blessed the earth.—The Complete Works of E.M. Bounds

Jonathan Edwards must be placed among the praying saints—one whom God mightily used through the instrumentality of prayer. As in the instance of the great New Englander, purity of heart should be ingrained in the very foundation of every man who is a true leader of his fellow men and a minister of the Gospel of Christ and who a constantly practiced the holy office of prayer. A sample of the utterances of this mighty man of God is here given in the shape of a resolution which he formed, and wrote down:

"Resolved," he says, "to exercise myself in this all my life long, viz., with the greatest openness to declare my ways to God, and to lay my soul open to God—all my sins, temptations, difficulties, sorrows, fears, hopes, desires, and everything and every circumstance."

We are not surprised, therefore, that the result of such fervid and honest praying was to lead him to record in his diary:

"It was my continual strife day and night, and my constant inquiry how I should be more holy, and live more holy. The heaven I desired was a heaven of holiness. I went on with my eager pursuit after more holiness and conformity to Christ."

The character and work of Jonathan Edwards were exemplifications of the great truth that the ministry of prayer is the efficient agency in every truly God-ordered work and life. He himself gives some particulars about his life when as a boy. He might well be called the "Isaiah of the Christian dispensation." There was united in him great mental powers, ardent piety, and devotion to study, unequaled save by his devotion to God. Here is what he says about himself:

"When a boy I used to pray five times a day in secret, and to spend much time in religious conversation with other boys. I used to meet with them to pray together. So it is God's will through His wonderful grace, that the prayers of His saints should be one great and principal means of carrying on the designs of Christ's kingdom in the world. Pray much for the ministers and the Church of God."

The great powers of Edwards' mind and heart were exercised to procure an agreed union in extraordinary prayer of God's people everywhere. His life, efforts, and his character are an exemplification of his statement.

"The heaven I desire," he says, *"is a heaven spent with God; an eternity spent in the presence of divine love, and in holy communion with Christ."*

At another time he said:

"The soul of a true Christian appears like a little white flower in the spring of the year, low and humble on the ground, opening its bosom to receive the pleasant beams of the sun's glory, rejoicing as it were in a calm rapture, diffusing around a sweet fragrance, standing peacefully and lovingly in the midst of other flowers."

Again he writes:

"Once as I rode out in the woods for my health, having alighted from my horse in a retired place, as my manner has been to walk for divine contemplation and prayer, I had a view, that for me was extraordinary, of the glory of the Son of God as Mediator between God and man, and of His wonderful, great, full, pure, and sweet grace and love, and His meek and gentle condescension. This grace that seemed so calm and sweet, appeared also great above the heavens. The person of Christ appeared ineffably excellent with an excellency

great enough to swallow up all thought and conception, which continued, as near as I can judge, about an hour. It kept me the greater part of the time in a flood of tears and weeping aloud. I felt an ardency of soul to be, what I know not otherwise how to express, emptied and annihilated, to lie in the dust; to be full of Christ alone, to love Him with my whole heart." It would be selfish on my part not to pinpoint this humble man of the apostolic age.

—The Complete Works of E. M. Bounds

John Knox

The man with a message speaks to men, but he speaks in the presence of God. It was said of John Knox, as they buried him, "Here lies one who feared God so much that he never feared the face of any man."

When John Knox was standing for his principles against Queen Mary, she demanded whether he thought it right that the authority of rulers should be resisted. His answer was: "If princes exceed their bounds, madam, they may be resisted and even deposed." The world owes much to the great men who took their lives in their hands and had the courage to tell even kings and queens that there is a moral law which they break at their peril. — Barclay's Daily Study Bible (NT)

The Queen of Scots professed she was more afraid of the prayers of Mr. Knox, than of an army of ten thousand men. *John Flavel.*—The Treasury of David (by Charles Spurgeon).

It is said of Polycarp that when brought before the judge, and commanded to abjure and blaspheme Christ, he firmly answered, "Eighty and six years have I served him, and he never did me wrong, how then can I blaspheme my king who hath saved me?" He was then adjudged to the flames, and suffered cheerfully for Christ his Lord and Master—Adam Clarke's Commentary

A woman of prayer and of great devotion, who understands the meaning of earnest in prayer. Who can look at death in the face and not even bring a tear to the eyes. "Blandina, on the day when she was first brought into the amphitheater, she was suspended on a piece of wood fixed in the ground, and exposed as food for the wild beasts; at which time, by her earnest prayers, she encouraged others. But none of the wild beasts would touch her, so that she was remanded to prison. When she was again produced for the third and last time, she was accompanied by Ponticus, a youth of fifteen, and the constancy of their faith so enraged the multitude that neither the sex of the one nor the youth of the other were respected, being exposed to all manner of punishments and tortures. Being strengthened by Blandina, he persevered unto death; and she after enduring all the torments heretofore mentioned, was at length slain with the sword." Beloved, prayer was the weapon that kept this godly woman through the ordeal of death.
—Foxe's Book of Christian Martyrs

As it was with Jonathan Edwards, so it is with all great intercessors. They come into that holy and elect condition of mind and heart by a thorough self-dedication to God, by periods of God's revelation to them, making distinct marked eras in their spiritual history—eras never to be forgotten. These are times in which faith mounts up with wings as eagles, and brings a new and fuller vision of God, a stronger grasp of faith, a sweeter, clearer vision of all things heavenly and eternal, and a blessed intimacy with, and access to, God. He shows how these men based their entire Christian foundation on prayer and fasting; how the Lord in turn used them to reach and change a people and generation.

I personally loved the book and would recommend it to everyone. It's not just about prayer; it's about life and how to live it to the fullest. Even the heathen understand the importance of connecting oneself to a "higher power" in order to be successful in this life. Knowing that one could make his or her situation immensely better just by talking to God is a gift that shouldn't be withheld from anyone. Anyone breathing should read this book. I feel as though I've discovered prayer for the very first time after reading this book. Rather then falling in line with the rules and obligations of religion, I have found that I am actually paying more attention to my prayers—approach, content, etc—and have seen the effects, both good and bad, on a daily basis.

The Weapon of Prayer is just that: a weapon. It teaches the children of God how to and why one should remain in constant communication with the Lord. God is not looking for eloquence or art in the form of lip service. He is looking for true and faithful sons and daughters who will take the time and make the sacrifice to listen to what He has to say, and to tell Him in all honesty how they feel and what they want. The energy of prayer is beyond measure. There is no greater purpose for God's creation other than to remain in fervent conversation with its Creator. The Word says we were made to praise Him; to pray is to praise and worship him in the most absolute and simple way. Prayer is truly the ultimate weapon of spiritual warfare afforded to man.

CHAPTER TWO

THE PLACE OF FASTING

WHAT IS FASTING?

Fasting is the discipline of abstaining from food for biblical reasons. It is called "afflicting one's soul" (Isa. 58:3), and is
often practiced to demonstrate the sincerity of our prayers. There
are several biblical reasons for fasting. Christians should fast when
facing a national crisis (2 Chron. 20:3; Ezra 8:21; Esther. 4:16),
for individual needs (Matt. 17:21), during periods of distress (2
Sam. 3:35; Ps. 35:13), when facing spiritual decisions (Matt. 4:2;
Acts 13:2), and in anticipation of Christ's return (Luke 5:35).
Many people have found that heavy burdens are relieved through
fasting (Isa. 58), wisdom is obtained through fasting (Dan. 10),
revival comes from fasting (Isa. 58:6), God's protection from danger is secured by fasting (1 Kings 21:27–29), recovery of a sick
loved one may come after fasting (Ps. 35:13), and the inauguration of a great ministry may follow fasting (Matt. 4:2). (First
Reference, Judges 20:26; Primary Reference, Is. 58:6; cf. James
5:14).

Biblical fasting is partial or total abstinence from the natural carnal desires for the purpose of dedicating time to the spiritual growth of your inner man and the sharpening of your spiritual senses for spiritual warfare. It may be abstinence from:

a. Food (Luke 4:2)
b. Food and water (Esther 4:16)
c. Food and sex (1 Cor. 7:5)

In the Bible, most cases of fasting mean total abstinence from food and we will limit ourselves here to this definition. In fact, water is not food, and unless specifically stated in the Bible, was always taken in abundance during a fast. Any nourishment taken—food or drink, other than water—during a fast breaks the fast, and therefore should not be called a fast, but rather a diet. Under no conditions should coffee, tea, chewing gum, or any other stimulant be taken during a fast.

WATER:
Water is the most important ingredient in our life. It's amazing that we have so overlooked the value and importance of drinking water. Water is a necessity of life. God the Father said to Moses in Deuteronomy 8:7, "For the Lord your God is bringing you into a good land, a land with streams of water, springs, and deep water sources, flowing in both valleys and hills…" (HCSB). And the Lord Jesus Christ the Eternal Son of God gave us a greater analogy of water by saying, "On the last day, the climax of the festival, Jesus stood and shouted to the crowds, 'If you are thirsty, come to me! If you believe in me, come and drink! For the Scriptures declare that rivers of living water will flow out from within.' (When he said 'living water,' he was speaking of the Spirit, who would be given to everyone believing in him. But the Spirit had not yet been given, because Jesus had not yet entered into his glory)" (John 7:37-39, NLT). God knows how important water is to our existence; in both the Old Testament and New

Testament covenants He emphasized it.

Let's look at some scientific facts about water:

The average adult human body contains about forty-five quarts of water.

Ninety-two percent of the human blood is made up of water.

Water makes up sixty-five percent of the human body.

The temperature of the body is controlled through water.

Water makes intestinal, gastric, saliva, and pancreatic juices.

Water prevents dehydration resulting in parched, dry skin, chronic constipation, and burning, irritating urine.

Water holds all nutritive factors in solution and acts as a transportation medium to various parts of the body.

Water keeps mucous membranes soft and free from friction. For those of us who drink too little water, we will likely suffer from constipation and increase our risk of heat exhaustion or even heat stroke. Lack of water can also make us more susceptible to asthma attacks, dental disease, kidney stones, and urinary tract infection. We need to drink six to eight glasses of water per day. Many experts disagree over what kind of water we should drink. Some say we should drink mineral water fresh from unpolluted springs. But Dr. Norman Walker in his book, Water Can Undermine Your Health, recommends drinking distilled water because it helps to cleanse inorganic mineral deposits that are of no constructive value to the body. He writes, "…distilled water collects the minerals discarded…originally collected from its contact with the earth and rocks." But to me, I experience both distilled and spring water. My conclusion in this matter is this: If God said it in the Old Testament and Jesus revisited it in the New Testament, it is extremely important that we drink water, especially during periods of fasting.

Fasting enhances the speedy release of power. It is not begging God to act, but getting empowered to deal with situations of life. It is a spiritual device for receiving the anointing.

Isaiah 58 lays out the pattern of the fast that is acceptable to God, its purpose, and what it is designed to accomplish. "*Is not this the fast that I have chosen? To loose the bands of wickedness, to undo the heavy burdens, and to let the oppressed go free, and that ye break every yoke?*" The motive for fasting must be a heart full of love for the salvation of lost souls. Then God will work as your prayer and fasting increases in intensity. We also discovered several scriptural objectives for fasting God's way:

A. To humble ourselves
B. To come closer to God
C. To help us understand God's word
D. To find God's will and to receive direction in our lives
E. To seek healing or deliverance from evil spirits
F. To seek God's intervention in some particular crisis or some problem which cannot be handled by ordinary means
G. To intercede and pray on behalf of others
H. To loose the bands of wickedness
I. To undo the heavy burdens
J. To let the oppressed go free
K. And to break every yoke.

Who has the courage to say that there is no need in the world today for victory in these eleven areas—even in the Church? Instead of obedience to God's Word in prevailing prayer and fasting, many pastors and leaders today would rather leave their people bound, captive in anguish, or else send them to worldly, godless doctors and psychologists who bleed them of their money that should have been for the betterment of their family or given to the church to proclaim the gospel.

"Isn't the fast I choose: To break the chains of wickedness, to untie the ropes of the yoke, to set the oppressed free, and to tear off every yoke?" (Isa. 58:6-7, HCSB).

This is the purpose for every fast. But some people have mistaken fasting to mean the affliction of the soul, or the subduing of the flesh.

The fast I mean here is that which endues one with power from on high, one that breaks yokes (you know the anointing destroys yokes). It is not one in which you pray, "Oh God, deal with all the witches in my city." The fast I'm talking about here is one in which God supernaturally empowers you to destroy all yokes—not Him doing it for you. That is why Isaiah declares, "And it shall come to pass in that day, that his burden shall be taken away from off thy shoulder, and his yoke from off thy neck; and the yoke shall be destroyed because of the anointing" (Isa. 10:27 Darby).

After Jesus was baptized in water, He was led by the Spirit into the wilderness, where He fasted for forty days. The Bible says He returned in the power of the Spirit into Nazareth and exploded! He was empowered for ministry after His fast. Jesus made it plain that fasting is not meant for struggling with the devil, but for enduement with power, so we can deal with the devil.

The purpose of fasting is to enhance your strength, so you can loose the bands of wickedness, undo the heavy burdens, and break every yoke. This is God's kind of fast.

I do not believe that fasting is essentially meant for getting answers to prayer. Whenever we pray according to His will, He is committed to answer. Many of the things you fast and pray about will not need prayer when you are empowered; they will answer to you automatically, because you will have authority to command them at will. There is a realm of power in which to operate, where even your presence is an answer in itself. Satan sees you, recognizes you as his tormentor, and cries out, "Jesus, I know, Paul I know." When you engage in this God-ordained fast, you build yourself up spiritually to a point where Satan steers clear of you and the issues that concern you.

After I ministered at a crusade sometime in 2001, there was great demonstration of power at the end of the meeting. That night when I went home to sleep, I awakened just twenty minutes later out of a deep dream. In the dream, I saw a human-like beast flying up and down with a black skirt and a red shirt, and her hair was braided like a dreadlock, each braid had the appearance of a snake. That very day a lady who had come from Paris had been wearing that same outfit and she had wanted to have a relationship with me. I know that was the work of the devil. I did not say a word to her because I had built myself up spiritually to the point where whatever the enemy would come up with I could detect. Why? Because I was doing what God required of me. When she insisted and I did not answer her advances, she went and blasted me in front of the church, but to God be the glory, my friend, Clervil, was there to witness the whole thing. It did not disturb me at all. Why? I had built myself up to a point where Satan was no longer a concern to me. You, too, can build up your power system to a point where anything that comes your way can be dealt with without you having to run in confusion.

"Then shall thy light break forth as the morning, and thine health shall spring forth speedily: and thy righteousness shall go before

thee; the glory of the Lord shall be thy reward. Then shalt thou call, and the Lord shall answer; thou shalt cry, and he shall say, here I am. If thou take away from the midst of thee the yoke, the putting forth of the finger, and speaking vanity..." (Isa. 58:8-9, AKJV).

These are some of the things that happen after you have been empowered. I call them spiritual goodies:

A. Light will break forth like the rising sun
B. Healing will quickly appear
C. Righteousness will go before you
D. Glory of the Lord will be your rear guard
E. Answered prayer—the Lord will answer when you cry for help
F. Continual guidance—the Lord will guide you always
G. Satisfaction—He will satisfy your needs
H. Refreshing—you will be like a well-watered garden
I. Vigor—He will strengthen your frame
J. Work that endures—repairer of broken walls
K. Restoration—restorer of streets with dwellings

"You shall call, and the Lord shall answer..." That connotes authority.

If God answers your call, then everything else is at your command. All you need do is say it, and it answers to you.

The essence of fasting is to build you up in power, not for you to lose weight or to look exhausted. If fasting does not culminate in the release of unction, then all you engaged in was a hunger strike.

FASTING TO REFILL
"I have lived with weariness and pain and sleepless nights.

Often I have been hungry and thirsty and have gone without food. [Fasting often] Often I have shivered with cold, without enough clothing to keep me warm" (2 Cor. 11:27, NLT).

Paul saw fasting as a means of increasing his power level. He fasted often and had proofs of his encounters with unction. It was not just something he did out of a religious mentality. Paul grew up in power to the extent that people said of him, "When the crowd saw what Paul had done, they went wild, calling out in their Lyconian dialect, 'The gods have come down! These men are gods!' " (Acts 14:11, MSG). We fast in order that unbelievers will see the glory of God in our life, and so that we can free them from their distress and heavy burdens.

Just as you would refill a lamp when its oil level had gone down, you need to refill your power supply constantly through fasting. When you observe your power gauge and see that your power supply is running out, you need to go on a fast to refill it.

Perhaps you sing and you sense that you are disconnected, or you pray but are not getting through. You might also feel that there is no trace of eternal life flowing in you. You need to go to the filling station for a refill. Look at fasting periods as opportunities to grow in the anointing, because it is during these times you are reconnected to your power source and receive a fresh supply.

This is where accepting responsibility comes in. The anointing you need can only be acquired personally. Nobody can give you of his own. Spiritually, we are like cars with deep fuel tanks. Such tanks are designed in a way that once fuel goes into it, you can't get it out again. Likewise, nobody can give you some of his unction; each man must personally acquire his own. *All the bridesmaids got up and prepared their lamps. Then the five foolish*

ones asked the others, 'Please give us some of your oil because our
lamps are going out.' 'Go to a shop and buy some for yourselves' "
(Matt. 25:7-9, NLT).

WARRING WITH THE WORD

When Jesus was on a fast, I believe He must have been busy filling Himself with the Word of God, so that when it was time for battle, He could fight valiantly, using the Word as His weapon. He kept saying, *"It is written,"* until the devil fled.

"Now Jesus, full of the Holy Spirit, left the Jordan and was led by the Spirit into the wild.

For forty wilderness days and nights he was tested by the Devil. He ate nothing during those days, and when the time was up he was hungry.

The Devil, playing on his hunger, gave the first test: 'Since you're God's Son, command this stone to turn into a loaf of bread.'

Jesus answered by quoting Deuteronomy [8:3]: 'It takes more than bread to really live.'

For the second test he led him up and spread out all the kingdoms of the earth on display at once.

Then the Devil said, 'They're yours in all their splendor to serve your pleasure. I'm in charge of them all and can turn them over to whomever I wish.

Worship me and they're yours, the whole works.'

Jesus refused, again backing his refusal with Deut. [6:13; 10:20]: '"Worship the Lord your God and only the Lord your God. Serve him with absolute single-heartedness."'

For the third test the Devil took him to Jerusalem and put him on top of the Temple. He said, [Ps. 91:11-12] 'If you are God's Son, jump.

It's written, isn't it, that "he has placed you in the care of angels to protect you;

they will catch you; you won't so much as stub your toe on a stone?" '

'Yes,' said Jesus, [Deut.6: 16] 'and it's also written,' "Don't you dare tempt the Lord your God." ' "

That completed the testing. The Devil retreated temporarily, lying in wait for another opportunity" (Luke 4:1-13, MSG). Realize the enemy always stands by waiting for other opportunities.

There may be some contrary circumstances fighting against you right now, for which you will need more unction than you presently have. Jesus prescribed a remedy for such situations: "So Jesus said to them, *Because of your unbelief; for assuredly, I say to you, if you have faith as a mustard seed, you will say to this mountain, 'Move from here to there,' and it will move; and nothing will be impossible for you. However, this kind does not go out except by prayer and fasting"* (Matt. 17:20-21).

Fasting is for spiritual empowering. If it does not culminate in the release of power, it's a waste of energy.

CHAPTER THREE

PRAYER AND FASTING
IN THE
OLD TESTAMENT

A study of the Old Testament shows that God places equal importance on both prayer and fasting. "This is standard practice for you, a perpetual ordinance. On the tenth day of the seventh month, both the citizen and the foreigner living with you are to enter into a solemn fast and refrain from all work, because on this day atonement will be made for you, to cleanse you. In the presence of God you will be made clean of all your sins [Heb 10:1, 2; 1 John1:7,9]. It is a Sabbath of all Sabbaths. You must fast. It is a perpetual ordinance" (Lev. 16:29-31, MSG).

The priest had his duties to perform and the people had their duties. The priest's duty was to go into the Holy of Holies with the blood of the sacrifice and make propitiation for the sins of the people. However, the people had their part to do, and that was twofold:
   A. To fast
   B. To abstain from all work

If prayer and fasting was not an option for physical Israel, it is not an option for the spiritual Israel. Also, we see that when prayer was accompanied by fasting, God moved in power to answer those prayers.

In the ninth chapter of Deuteronomy Moses gave us a very important example of fasting. Moses fasted a second forty days and forty nights. "Then, for another forty days and nights I lay before the Lord, neither eating bread nor drinking water, for you had done what the Lord hated most, thus provoking him to great anger" (Deut 9:18 TLB).

MOSES
The first occasion of Moses' lengthy fast was when he was on the mount with God, when at the end he received the two tablets of the law. In the case to which we call special attention, Moses had come down from the mount with the tablets of the law and discovered Israel's sinful worship of the golden calf. He destroyed that idol, and was now pleading with the Lord Jehovah to spare the lives of sinful Israel, whom God had declared He was about to destroy. Moses had no promise here to plead. On the contrary, he had a distinct prohibition against asking for the remission of the decree of destruction. "Let me alone," declared Jehovah. This was evidently a reply to the importunities of Moses, who for forty days with unappeased appetite pressed his case. God finally granted his prayer. Note the means by which this man of God secured his petition—by prayer and fasting—the very thing that millions of professing Christians today do not do.

ISAIAH
The Prophet Isaiah left the people of God with what may be considered the Magna Charta of Fasting. In Isaiah chapter 58, we have a series of promises and objectives for those who fast according to the will of God. I truly believe I will do the body of

Christ a disservice if I omit looking at some of these statements. The Lord assured us that all of these promises are ours if we fast based according to what the prophet Isaiah prescribed. "Then shall thy light break forth as the morning, and thine health shall spring forth speedily: and thy righteousness shall go before thee; the glory of the LORD shall be thy rearward. Then shalt thou call, and the LORD shall answer; thou shall cry, and he shall say, Here I am. If thou take away from the midst of thee the yoke, the putting forth of the finger, and speaking vanity; And if thou draw out thy soul to the hungry, and satisfy the afflicted soul; then shall thy light rise in obscurity, and thy darkness be as the noonday: And the LORD shall guide thee continually, and satisfy thy soul in drought, and make fat thy bones: and thou shall be like a watered garden, and like a spring of water, whose waters fail not. And they that shall be of thee shall build the old waste places: thou shall raise up the foundations of many generations; and thou shall be called, the repairer of the breach..." (Isa. 58:8-12).

EZRA
Fasting and Prayer for Protection

In the eighth chapter of the book of Ezra we encounter this beautiful statement. "Then I proclaimed a fast there at the river of Ahava, that we might humble ourselves before our God, to seek from Him the right way for us and our little ones and all our possessions" (Ezra 8:21).

We have another instance of how quickly the ancient people of God resorted to fasting and prayer as the means of releasing God's omnipotent hand. Ezra, the divinely chosen man to lead the return of captive Israel from Babylon to their ancient home Jerusalem, had gathered some forty thousand men, women, and children. The king of Babylon had bestowed a great deal of riches upon them in order to enable them to rebuild the city of Jerusalem. With great joy they marched through the king's domain until they came to its boundaries. There they faced the unbroken wilderness, infested with criminals and robbers. They themselves were wholly unarmed. What should they do? They immediately resorted to the method their fathers had frequently employed with such a signal success. They called for a period of fasting—the very thing that is so universally unknown among Christians today. Here where thousands of men, women, and children were wholly unarmed, they were loaded with unusual treasures and spoil—a helpless company loaded with rich booty for bandits and robbers. They sincerely fasted and God's power was released upon them so that they were able to travel safely to their destination. They used the very means of securing His favor and releasing His power that today is generally thought not necessary. Is not the God of today the same as He who guided and protected the Israelites when they were traveling back to build their fallen capital? Who, then, can tell the wondrous revivals that would take place, the individual conversions that would occur, and the release of God's power that could be had in these days, if his people would more faithfully practice this biblical method of carrying on His work?

NEHEMIAH

In the first chapter of Nehemiah, we have an instance where that man of God was praying and fasting over the unbuilt walls of his people's capital city. "So it was, when I heard these words, that I sat down and wept, and mourned for many days; I was fasting and praying before the God of heaven. And I said: 'I pray, LORD God of heaven, O great and awesome God, You who keep Your covenant and mercy with those who love You and observe Your commandments, please let Your ear be attentive and Your eyes open, that You may hear the prayer of Your servant which I pray before You now, day and night, for the children of Israel Your servants, and confess the sins of the children of Israel which we have sinned against You. Both my father's house and I have sinned. We have acted very corruptly against You, and have not kept the commandments, the statutes, nor the ordinances which You commanded Your servant Moses. Remember, I pray, the word that You commanded Your servant Moses, saying, "If you are unfaithful, I will scatter you among the nations; but if you return to Me, and keep My commandments and do them, though some of you were cast out to the farthest part of the heavens, yet I will gather them from there, and bring them to the place which I have chosen as a dwelling for My name." ' 'Now these are Your servants and Your people, whom You have redeemed by Your great power, and by Your strong hand. O Lord, I pray, please let Your ear be attentive to the prayer of Your servant, and to the prayer of Your servants who desire to fear Your name; and let Your servant prosper this day, I pray, and grant him mercy in the sight of this man' " (Neh 1:4-11).

As a result of Nehemiah's prayer and fasting, God moved upon the heart of the king, whom Nehemiah served as a cupbearer, and was sent to Jerusalem to supervise the reconstruction of the ruined walls of the city. Here again, this man also obtained the answer to his prayers by means of fasting. God's protection from danger is secured by fasting (1 Kings 21:27–29).

ESTHER

In the book of Esther we are told that the king, without knowing that Esther was a Jewess, had chosen this beautiful young woman as the queen of his empire. At the same time the wicked Haman, who hated the Israelites, had conspired with success to secure a decree from the King for the concerted destruction of all the Jews in the kingdom. Mordecai, Esther's relative and guardian, congratulated her upon being chosen queen, for that would, he declared, enable her to importune the king for the remission of the fatal decree that called for the death of all the Jews. Esther sent back word that until the King officially sent for her it was fatal for her to attempt to talk with him, and that she dared not force herself upon him. To this Mordecai answered that she would die anyway, for when the fatal day fixed by the decree should dawn, the executioners would learn that she was a Jewess, and, consequently, she would be included in the massacre. Upon receiving this statement, the queen replied: "Go and gather together all the Jews of Susa and fast for me. Do not eat or drink for three days, night or day. My maids and I will do the same. And then, though it is against the law, I will go in to see the king. If I must die, I am willing to die" (Esther 4:16, TLB).

The result of this general fast on the part of the Jews was that God touched the heart of the king, gave Esther favor with Him, induced him to remember the good office of Mordecai which had been rendered to the realm on a previous occasion, and caused a fall-out with Haman, the instigator of the plot. Whereupon the king sent Haman to the gallows which Haman himself had erected for the expected execution of Mordecai, whom he especially hated. They were all freed from the decree. How did it happen? Fasting! Victory from fasting (Isa. 58: 6).

JOEL

In the book of Joel, the prophet states that when the times are desperate God himself exhorts His people to seek aid from Him, and suggests how to come to him: "...Come with fasting, weeping, mourning. Let your remorse tear at your hearts and not your garments." Return to the Lord your God, for he is gracious and merciful. He is not easily angered; he is full of kindness and anxious not to punish you.

"Who knows? Perhaps even yet He will decide to leave you alone and give you a blessing instead of his terrible curse. Perhaps He will give you so much that you can offer your grain and wine to the Lord as before!" (Joel 2:12-14, TLB).

"And also you priests, put on your robes and join the outcry. You who lead people in worship, lead them in lament. Spend the night dressed in gunnysacks, you servants of my God. Nothing's going on in the place of worship, no offerings, no prayers—nothing.

Declare a holy fast, call a special meeting, get the leaders together, Round up everyone in the country. Get them into God's Sanctuary for serious prayer to God.

What a day! Doomsday! God's Judgment Day has come. The Strong God has arrived. This is serious business!

Food is just a memory at our tables, as are joy and singing from God's Sanctuary.

The seeds in the field are dead, barns deserted, Grain silos abandoned. Who needs them? The crops have failed!

The farm animals groan—oh, how they groan! The cattle mill around. There's nothing for them to eat. Not even the sheep find anything.

God! I pray, I cry out to you! The fields are burning up, The country is a dust bowl, forest and prairie fires rage unchecked" (Joel 1:13-19, MSG).

Would not many of the perilous times faced by God's people in the past few years have ended in joyous and flaming revival if this biblical method had been followed?

JONAH

In the prophet Jonah's day, the king and the people of Nineveh were alarmed on account of his preaching of an eight-word sermon. "Then the word of the LORD came to Jonah a second time: 'Go to the great city of Nineveh and proclaim to it the message I give you.'

"Jonah obeyed the word of the LORD and went to Nineveh. Now Nineveh was a very important city—a visit required three days. On the first day, Jonah started into the city. He proclaimed: 'Forty more days and Nineveh will be overturned.' The Ninevites believed God. They declared a fast, and all of them, from the greatest to the least, put on sackcloth.

"When the news reached the king of Nineveh, he rose from his throne, took off his royal robes, covered himself with sackcloth and sat down in the dust. Then he issued a proclamation in Nineveh:

'By the decree of the king and his nobles:

'Do not let any man or beast, herd or flock, taste anything; do not let them eat or drink. But let man and beast be covered with sackcloth. Let everyone call urgently on God. Let them give up their evil ways and their violence' " (Jonah 3:1-8, NIV). God wanted to destroy Nineveh because of their wickedness and violence. These are the same sins that ravage our the world today.

The response of the people was so remarkable. What did God do for them? "When God saw what they did and how they turned from their evil ways, he had compassion and did not bring upon them the destruction he had threatened" (Jonah 3:10, NIV).

"That is why the Lord says, 'Turn to me now, while there is time! Give me all your hearts. Come with fasting, weeping, mourning' " (Joel 2: 12, TLB).

I could think of no better way to secure the intervention of God in their behalf, and the answer to their prayers, than to fast. And God answered their prayers, saving the entire city for almost two hundred years before Nineveh was finally destroyed.

CHAPTER FOUR

PRAYER AND FASTING
IN THE
NEW TESTAMENT

The New Testament gives consistent testimony to the importance of prayer and fasting, both in the life and teaching of Jesus, as well as of His disciples. Jesus began His ministry by prayer and fasting for forty days. "Jesus prepared for the Test by fasting forty days and forty nights. That left him, of course, in a state of extreme hunger" (Matt 4:2, MSG). And the inauguration of a great ministry may follow fasting.

During that time He was attacked by the arch-enemy of our souls—the devil himself. Jesus was fiercely assaulted and tempted in the three areas which we also must overcome: the flesh, the world, and the devil. Note that Jesus prepared Himself for the attack in these three areas by prayer and fasting. He used the written word of God and overcame all three areas of temptation in this order: the flesh, the world, and the devil. Many Christians live for weeks and months under oppression. All spiritual oppression is caused by demon spirits. Jesus stated that deliverance from some kinds of demons only comes by prayer and fasting. "But this kind does not go out but by prayer and fasting" (Matt. 17:21, Darby).

Not prayer alone—but with fasting. Fasting is for the purpose of raising the level of your faith to the point where God can do through you what He could not do otherwise. Some Christians would rather remain under the heel of the oppressor than to obey Christ in fasting and prayer until the power of the oppressor is broken. Many fear the reprimand and mocking of a few well-meaning "ministers" and relatives rather than fear the Lord and His commandments. Some people say: "I'll fast when God puts it on me." They also only pray when God "puts it on them," and their spiritual life is their testimony of unbelief and disorderliness. They don't wait until God "puts it on them" to go to work, or to eat. They eat three times a day regularly. God expects us to have orderly lives, but He expects us to have orderly spiritual lives also.

Church history tells us that the first-century Christians literally ran the church with periods of fasting. In Acts 13:2, we encounter this wonderful experience and this should be the everyday experience of the church today. Note that there were just five people in the local fellowship and as they ministered unto the Lord and fasted, the Holy Spirit said, "Separate me Barnabas and Saul for the work whereunto I have called them" (AKJV). Then the bible does not say if it was days or weeks later: "And when they had fasted and prayed, and laid their hands on them, they sent them away, so they, being sent forth by the Holy Ghost...." Acts 13:3 (AKJV). For the first two centuries most Christians fasted regularly two days a week—Tuesdays and Fridays. What life would flow through the body of Christ today if all sincere Christians would unite their hearts throughout the world and dedicate two days a week to prayer and fasting for world revival and the salvation of the lost! Nevertheless, God will also hold each of us accountable for this spiritual exercise.

CHAPTER FIVE

THE *BASICS* OF *FASTING*

A. 10 REASONS FOR FASTING

1. To minister unto the Lord (Acts 13:2, 3).

2. To increase our faith (Matt. 17:19-21). "And nothing shall be impossible unto you." During the fast some people have visions of heaven and glory and angels and it greatly increases their faith. "I will cause thee to ride upon the high places of the earth" (Isa. 58:14).

3. To give ourselves to prayer (1 Cor. 7:5).

4. To walk in the Spirit. "There is therefore now no condemnation to those who are in Christ Jesus, who do not walk according to the flesh, but according to the Spirit" (Rom. 8:1).

The Bible teaches that there is a continuous conflict between the flesh and the Spirit, i.e., between our natural desires and the Spirit of the Lord. Until you have fasted two or three weeks you shall never know how much your old man nature still needs to be crucified. It is during the fast that weaknesses, hidden sins, and fleshly desires are revealed. Mortify [put to death] therefore your members which are upon the earth; fornication, uncleanness, inordinate affection, evil concupiscence, and covetousness, which is idolatry..." (Col. 3:5, AKJV).

5. Fasting brings heart-faith to believe the words and promises of Jesus. Most Christians believe sincerely with their minds, but there is a heart-faith that brings miracles. "...And shall not doubt in his heart, but shall believe those things which he saith shall come to pass, he shall have whatsoever he saith" (Mark 11:23, AKJV). The closer you draw to Jesus the more you will be able to believe and receive from Him. "The word is nigh thee, even in thy mouth, and in thy heart: that is, the word of faith" (Rom. 10:8). ..."For with the heart man believeth..." (Rom. 10:10)... "All things are possible to him who believes..." (Mark 9:23). "If you have faith...nothing shall be impossible for you" (Matt. 17:20).

6. To have faith to pray for the sick, to lay hands on them and see them healed, delivered from demon oppression. Faith to see your husband saved or rebellious wife brought to Jesus. Faith to see your broken home reunited. Faith to believe Jesus Christ, nothing shall be impossible for you. (Matt. 17:20).

7. To obtain faith to be used by the Lord for the salvation of souls. It is impossible to say that we are following the Lord Jesus if we are not winning souls unto Him. For He said: "Follow me and I will make you to become fishers of men" (Mark 1:17). Souls won to the Lord Jesus Christ, not to my group or my ideas, but to Him. Fasting with prayer is not biblical if it is not accompanied by an intense heart desire to see men, women, boys and girls born into the kingdom of God; truly delivered out of the kingdom of

darkness and translated into the kingdom of God's dear Son (Col. 1:13). This demands the utmost effort on our part. The Kingdom of God suffers violence and the violent take it by force (Matt. 11:12). It is impossible to spoil the house of the strongman (the devil) unless he first be bound by prayer and fasting (Matt. 12:29). Most Christians float for years, many all their lives in a half-dead condition, without being able to say that they have won one soul to the Lord. Fervent intercessory prayer with fasting will break these chains of indifference, laziness, and desperation and trans-form your life into a firebrand in the hand of the Lord. That is why God said this to Micah in response to the children of Israel's search on how to serve God.

> "You say, 'What can I bring with me
>   when I come before the Lord,
>   when I bow before God on high?
> Should I come before him with burnt offerings,
>   with year-old calves?
> Will the Lord be pleased with a thousand male sheep?
> Will he be pleased with ten thousand rivers of oil?
> Should I give my first child for the evil I have done?
> Should I give my very own child for my sin?'
> But God said to the Prophet, this is what I required.
> "The Lord has told you, human, what is good;
>   he has told you what he wants from you:
>   to do what is right to other people,
>   love being kind to others,
>   and live humbly, obeying your God" (Micah 6:6-8, NCV).

8. Fasting will bring you faith to be filled with the Holy Spirit and to stay filled with the Holy Spirit, so that the Holy Spirit may live His life in and through you. The normal life of the Holy Spirit in you is presented in 1 Corinthians 12, as nine gifts or manifestations of the Holy Spirit flowing through you. These

gifts or manifestations are not yours, nor your property; they belong exclusively to the Holy Spirit (1 Cor. 12:11), and He manifests through each person as He wants.

Many people fast and pray for the gifts or "gift" given to them so that they can "use" them the way they want to. It is not he who uses God that shall be approved, but He whom God uses. "Knowing the correct password—saying 'Master, Master,' for instance—isn't going to get you anywhere with me. What is required is serious obedience—doing what my Father wills.

I can see it now—at the Final Judgment thousands strutting up to me and saying, 'Master, we preached the Message, we bashed the demons, our God-sponsored projects had everyone talking.'

And do you know what I am going to say? 'You missed the boat. All you did was use me to make yourselves important. You don't impress me one bit. You're out of here' " (Matt. 7:21-23).

We should seek all the gifts or manifestations of the Holy Spirit, but at the same time realize that it is His normal life which is flowing through us, and the purpose of the Holy Spirit is to ever glorify Jesus (John 16:4). You must be filled with the Holy Spirit initially in order for the nine gifts to begin flowing in your life. A Christian receives the baptism in the Holy Spirit in the same way he accepts the Lord Jesus Christ as his own personal Savior by faith. The way to receive the baptism in the Holy Spirit is to get your knees, lift your hands to God in an act of faith receiving. Then start praising the Lord with all your heart in thanksgiving for so great a salvation and for the precious blood of Jesus that has cleaned you from all sin. Thank Him out loud that you are a Son of God through the wonderful finished work of Christ on the cross for you, until the Lord Jesus fills you with His love, joy unspeakable and peace. Jesus will then give you a new tongue with which to praise God. Speak it by faith and the Holy Spirit will build you up spiritually (1 Cor.14: 4), so that the other eight manifestations of the Holy Spirit will also begin to flow through you—the word of wisdom, word of knowledge, discerning of spirits, prophecy, tongues, miracles, faith, and gifts of healing. Jesus said these signs would follow the believer; that is, each one who believes or who is a true Christian.

The gifts of the spirit are not for a "special group" of Christians, but are for every believer. In my Name they shall cast out devils, they shall speak new tongues, they shall lay hands on the sick and they shall recover (Mark 16:18). God is no respecter of persons (Gal 2:6). Claim your throne rights as soon as you receive the baptism in the Holy Spirit. Prayer and fasting open the door for the manifestations to flow in abundance (1 Cor. 14:12).

At salvation, the Holy Spirit baptizes you into the body of Christ (1 Cor. 12:13). In the Holy Ghost baptism, the Lord Jesus Christ baptizes you with the Holy Ghost and fire (Luke 3:16). "You shall receive power after that the Holy Ghost is come upon you: and you shall be witnesses unto me [The Lord Jesus]… (Acts 1:8, AKJV). Keep your eyes on Jesus and glorify Jesus in all that you do. God will never give a serpent to a son of His who asks for an egg. How much more shall the Holy Father give the Holy Spirit to His children who ask Him? (Luke 11:13).

Many Christians, who have received the baptism in the Holy Spirit, have long since let the fire go out. Consistent prayer and fasting in the Holy Ghost will rekindle this flame and keep it burning (Jude 20). The Holy Spirit is a person who loves you and is sent to comfort you. He can be quenched and grieved. A praying and fasting Christian who is continually sober and watching in the spirit will help to keep himself from falling. Give diligence to make your calling and election sure, for if you do these things you shall never fall (II Pet.1: 10). Prayer and fasting will help to stir up the gift that is in you (II Tim.1: 6), that you may begin to move against the enemy, to become a soul winner, to have faith to pray for the sick, to cast out demons, lay hands on the afflicted and those bound by vices and drugs and see them liberated by Jesus. You will have faith to pray for those seeking the salvation of their souls and to see the powers of hell shaken. Faith to stand upon the promise of Jesus, that the gates of hell will not prevail against His Church (Matt. 16:18).

God is looking for men and women in this hour who dare to stand upon His Word and not be moved by the rudiment of traditions, customs, rituals, modes, and vices of a corrupt society, but will act as the son of Issachar to discern the time and the season and stand in the gap for a generation, a people, a nation, and the world. To the Joshua generation, there is a call that has gone forth for us to speak loud enough to be heard and be bold as a lion so we can prepare a people for the ushering in of the great coming of our Lord and King.

9. Prayer with fasting is the most powerful armor that God has given, or placed in the arsenal, of each member of His body. After a twenty-one-day fast, you will realize for the first time the biblical authority you have over diseases, demons, over princes, and powers of the air, which Jesus has given you through His triumphant work on the cross in your behalf (Col. 2:15).

10. Fasting and prayer will give you faith in your own life to experience Isaiah 58:8-14. In these verses God promises you as the results of biblical fasting:
    a. Revival in your spirit.
    b. A new power of concentration in your mind.
    c. And to restored health to your body.

Praise the Lord!

B. THE DURATION OF FASTING

When a Christian fasts, he should begin with a short fast—one day from sundown to sundown—and attempt to spend time alone with God during the fast. (First Reference, Judg. 20:26; Primary Reference, Isa. 58:6; cf. James 5:14).

Part of a day can be found in the book of Daniel 6:18

One Day: Lev.23:27, Judges 20:26; 1 Sam 7:6; 1 Sam 14:24; Jer. 36:6; Neh. 9:1

Three Days: Esther 4:16; 1 Sam. 30:12; Matt. 15:32; Mark 8:2, 3; Acts 9:9

Seven Days: 1 Sam. 31:11-13; 1 Chr. 10:11, 12; 2 Sam. 12:15-18, 21-23

Fourteen Days: Acts 27:33

Twenty-One Days: Dan. 10:2, 3

Forty Days: Exodus 34:28; Deut. 9:9; Deut. 9:18; 1 Kings 19:8; Matt. 4:1, 2; Luke 4:1, 2

Each person must pray to the Lord and seek guidance on the length of the fast and how often. Whatever you do, keep your promise with the Lord. If you decide to fast one meal, do it unto the Lord. If you eat nothing for a period of 24 hours, it is a one-day fast. If you eat nothing for 72 hours, it is a three-day fast. Your need and desperation should influence the length of the fast. If you have a mountain to remove in your life or in the life of a loved one, you may determine to fast until the results come. Assurance of the recovery of a sick loved one may come after fasting (Ps.

35:13). I've known Christians to covenant with God to fast and pray until demons leave loved ones, until they are delivered and set free from the grip and the oppression of the enemy. And some continued in prayer and fasting for 7 days, 21 days, 40 days or until demons came out. The length of the fast then is determined by the burden for souls or for deliverance from sin, sickness or oppression. May God increase our burden to match His burden for the lost until we cry out like Joel. "Sanctify ye a fast, call a solemn assembly, gather the elders and all the inhabitants of the land into the house of the Lord your God, and cry unto the Lord. Alas for the day! for the day of the Lord is at hand, and as a destruction from the Almighty shall it come" (Joel 1: 14-15, AKJV).

C. BEGINNING YOUR FAST

The Bible teaches that the physical body is the temple of the Holy Spirit. "Do you not know that your body is a temple of the Holy Spirit within you, which you have from God? You are not your own; you were bought with a price. So glorify God in your body" (1 Cor. 6:19-20, RSV). And the Bible revealed that when Jesus died and shed His blood on Calvary, He redeemed not only our spirits and souls but also our bodies. That is why the Apostle Paul said, "Now may the God of peace make you holy in every way, and may your whole spirit and soul and body be kept blameless until that day when our Lord Jesus Christ comes again" (1Thess 5:23, NLT). God desires to live in us and that is why the book of Acts of the Apostles echoed these words, "However, the Most High doesn't live in temples made by human hands. As the prophet says,

'Heaven is my throne,
and the earth is my footstool.
Could you ever build me a temple as good as that?'

Asks the Lord.

'Could you build a dwelling place for me?

Didn't I make everything in heaven and earth?' (Acts 7:48-50 NLT).

When a Christian fasts, he should begin with a short fast—one day from sundown to sundown—and attempt to spend time alone with God during the fast.

A short fast of a day or two needs no special preparation, but should always be dedicated to the Lord. If the fast is four days or more some preparation should be made. The longer the fast, the more preparation should be made. If you are going on a fast for three weeks or longer, you should make preparation to go some place alone to rest and to give yourself to prayer and the reading of the Word of God. You may become very thin on a long fast and some well-meaning friends may make life unbearable for you by continually criticizing and speaking negatively to you regarding your condition.

Jesus went into the wilderness to be alone during the forty-day fast beginning His ministry. In the long fast, preparation is very important. No work should be done. A pleasant restful atmosphere should be sought. Pure drinking water should be available in abundance. Before starting a week or longer fast, eat only fresh fruits and or fresh vegetables for a few days before the fast to cleanse your system. Drink warm water with lemon juice mixed with honey; that will purify your body. Take a warm sponge bath at least every two days, as the body will start to eliminate many poisons through the pores of your skin. Your breath may have a terrible odor during the fast and become unbearable to others but if you use oxygen water with baking soda that will keep your breath fresh. This merely means that your body is cleansing itself of poisons accumulated for years and that you are receiving physical as well as spiritual benefits from your fasting. The first day or so you may have a lot of hunger, but after the third day, all hunger will leave and will not return until the fast is over.

CHAPTER SIX

SPIRITUAL GUIDELINES FOR FASTING

For maximum effectiveness during the fast, you should set yourself apart for three things:

a. Earnest prayer according to Isaiah 58
b. Personal heart-searching according to Ps. 139:23-24
c. Reading and meditating in the Word of God—Joshua 1:8

The Word of God is the ultimate weapon in prayer. If it has been written in our hearts, it will create an outpouring current of prayer that is full and irresistible. Promises stored in the heart are the fuel from which prayer receives life and warmth, just as the oil that is stored in the earth ministers to our comfort on stormy days and wintry nights. The Word of God is the food by which prayer is nourished and made strong. Like people, prayer cannot live by bread alone, "…but by every word that proceedeth out of the mouth of God" (Matt 4:4, AKJV).

Unless God's Word supplies the living forces of prayer—even earnest prayer—though it may even be strong and noisy in its urgency, is, in reality, flabby, lifeless, and empty. The absence of living force prayers can be traced to the absence of a constant supply of God's Word, which repairs the waste and renews life. Those who would learn to pray well must study God's Word and store it in their memory and heart.

When we consult God's Word, we find that no duty is more binding and more exacting than that of prayer. But we also discover there is no greater privilege and no habit more richly acknowledged by God. No promises are more radiant, more numerous, more definite, more often repeated than those that are attached to prayer. All things, whatsoever are received by prayer, because "all things whatsoever" are promised (Matt. 21:22). There is no limit to the provisions found in the promises of prayer, and nothing is excluded from its promises. "For everyone who asks receives" (Luke 11:10). The word of our Lord is to this all-embracing effect:

"IF ye shall ask any thing in my name, I will do it" (John 14:14, AKJV).

If you diligently give yourself to these three, the time will pass quickly, and the enemy will have little occasion to discourage you or distract you with thoughts of self.

Do not work during a long fast, but rise every morning, get dressed, and give yourself to prayer until time to go to bed, except for the usual siesta. You will have difficult days as the fasting and cleansing goes deeper. Headaches, nausea, vomiting, etc., merely mean that you desperately needed the fast, as your body is cleansing itself of poisons. You will have days when you feel wonderful and your mind will be clearer for Bible study and concentration than it was before. You may have the temptation to work, but do not do it on a long fast; rather give yourself to prayer and the Word.

Much prayer during the fast may change your entire life and cause you to be much more fruitful for the Lord Jesus. By prayer and fasting the giant of unbelief will be slain in your life and a strong faith to claim the promises of Jesus will be born in your heart.

There is a kind of prayer called the "fasting-prayer." When you desire something so much that you cannot eat, that desire becomes a heart cry with intercessions which cannot be uttered. It is a "fasting-prayer," when this deep desire is a continuous heart-cry for more communion with Jesus, the only one who has power to break every fetter, free friends from vices, and save the souls of loved ones.

A congregation can move powerfully as a loyal body of Christ by consistent prayer and fasting. Those congregations throughout the world that I have seen or heard moving in power against the enemy, casting out demons and consistently seeing miracles and healing in their midst are those which have continuous prayer and fasting. One or two persons in the group are fasting every day of the week. Others choose different days. If you want your fellowship to move out for God, start a chain of fasting and intercessory prayer. Fasting, just like prayer, can never be obligatory. Encourage one another continuously by love and example. You cannot expect others to fast and pray if you yourself are not willing to become part of the chain.

You should drink at least 8-10 glasses of pure water daily during the fast. If you go on a long fast and pure water is not available, it is best to plan to have distilled water available to last during the fast. As the fasting progresses your senses become very sensitive, and the water you normally drink may be so offensive that you cannot drink it or will throw it up. This may dehydrate your body and become dangerous because your body needs abundant water to cleanse itself of poisons. If the water cannot be kept down you may have to terminate the fast. Chlorine will disappear from water, if left sitting in an open bottle overnight. But other chemicals in the water may make it eventually impossible to drink. Rather than break the fast, it is better to have abundant pure water available. To go three days without water as occurred in the Book of Esther is not recommended, unless the situation is desperate and God plainly directs. One should never go more than three days without water. God does not want to destroy our bodies. He desires above all things our health (3 John 2). The cleansing of your body with pure water is a type of the cleansing of the Word of God. You need abundant pure water, especially during the fast to keep the poisons flushing through your body. Headaches and other problems will greatly be diminished if you drink plenty of water. It will be like soaking a sponge in water and then squeezing it out over and over again until it is completely clean.

B. PHYSICAL REACTIONS DURING THE FAST

Everyone is different and many people have hidden diseases in their bodies, which begin to be cleansed through fasting, so the reactions will be as varied as people. The more suffering during your fast, the greater was the need for you to fast. If you have lived many years dependent upon nicotine or caffeine as a stimulant, you will probably have strong headaches and nausea for the first couple of days, until the withdrawal symptoms are over. If you are addicted to white sugar and caffeine, the nausea and withdrawal symptoms may last for a week or more.

Do not be afraid of weight loss. Keep your eyes on Jesus and not on your weight. If it is a 3-day, 21-day, or 40-day fast, let the Lord be glorified in all you do, with thanksgiving. If you eat normally after the fast, you will keep your normal weight.

While you are fasting it is difficult to catch cold, but you should keep yourself warm at all times too conserve body energy.

Some nights you may find it impossible to sleep. This is because the loss of weight lets an excess of blood in the body. This excess of blood in the head may keep you from sleeping a few nights. So praise the Lord for the wonderful opportunity to spend those nights in prayer and communion with Him!

❧❧❧

WISDOM AND BENEFITS
OF FASTING

This is a very important aspect of fasting and we should not it take lightly, for we can lose a lot of the benefits from fasting if we break the fast unwisely. Many of us don't realize that the word "breakfast," which we still use in the English language, means the meal that we break a fast. Unfortunately, so many people eat so late at night they never have a fast to break. "Any meal with which a fast is broken" WEBSTER'S UNABRIDGED. After fasting, always begin with a glass of apple juice or Gatorade, rather than a light meal, even if you have fasted only a short time. Never break a fast with foods that are cooked, greasy, fat, or heavy. My advice is to start with a salad—lettuce and raw greens. It will help tremendously with the purging process taking place in your body.

Inasmuch as you are able, keep your promise to the Lord and fast as long as He has shown you. It is good to pray and determinc the length of the fast beforehand. The normal time to break your fast will be when natural hunger returns. This may not be for many weeks or after 40 days. Natural hunger will not return until after the body is cleansed of all poisons. Notice that natural hunger did not return to Jesus until after He had fasted 40 days (Luke 4:13).

Many people confuse starvation with fasting. Some folks think they will starve to death if they miss a meal. The only reason the stomach reacts violently when it is denied food for a day is because of the habit of being continually filled. After three days all hunger leaves and true hunger does not return until the fast is over. True hunger does not return in the stomach, but in the mouth and the throat. You will never mistake it. When true hunger returns, you must eat or the body will enter into the starvation period. Notice that the devil was not foolish enough to offer Jesus bread during the 40-day fast. But after the hunger returned, Jesus knew it was a matter of life or death to be tempted by the devil. "He ate nothing during those days, and when they were over he was hungry" (Luke 4:2, NAB). Jesus, your great Victor, will help you overcome in these three areas of temptation also.

If you are fasting for only a few days, you should break the fast with grape juice and fruit. If you are fasting for several weeks, more caution should be taken to break your fast. Drink fresh orange juice in a half glass of water every two hours for the first day. The next day, drink pure orange juice every two hours, and on the third day eat three meals of fresh fruit. The fourth day you may eat fruit and fresh vegetables. The longer the fast, the slower you should break it. Extreme caution should be taken not to overeat, especially the first few days, as the desire to eat may damage your body and destroy all the benefits of the fast.

The control and temperance you learn during the fast should be carried over into your everyday life after the fast. Under no conditions should you break a long fast with meat, sweets, bread, pasta, rice, or anything heavy. If you want good health, eliminate all white sugars, candies, greasy food, and chocolates from your diet. If you eat two meals a day consisting mostly of fresh fruit and fresh vegetables you will keep your normal weight and add many years to your life. Remember that your body is the temple of the Holy Spirit. "If any man defile the temple of God, him shall God destroy…" (1 Cor. 3:17, AKJV). "What? know ye not that your body is the temple of the Holy Ghost which is in you, which ye have of God, and ye are not your own? For ye are bought with a price: therefore glorify God in your body, and in your spirit, which are God's" (1 Cor. 6:19-20, AKJV).

Many people refuse to discern the Lord's body and because of this are weak and sickly and die before their time (1 Cor. 11:30). Many so-called " spiritual ones" will make fun of you and say that it does not matter what you take into your body. Some say the same thing is true with the mind—it is not important what the mind feeds on. But if your mind feeds on the filth of TV, novels, comics, etc., is it any wonder this generation is reaping young people who are lovers of their own selves, covetous, boasters, proud, disobedient to parents, unthankful, unholy, men acting and dressing like women, women acting and dressing like men, despisers of those who are good, heady, high-minded, lovers of pleasures more than lovers of God: having a form of godliness, but denying the power thereof. (2 Tim 3:5) You can be assured that this is true in all three areas—spirit, mind, and body. Whatever you feed your spirit, whatever you feed your mind, whatever you feed your body, that will you reap. "Be not deceived; God is not mocked: for whatsoever a man soweth, that should he also reap" (Gal. 6:7, AKJV).

Many well-meaning Christians are under the intoxicating effect of alcohol most of their lives! Alcohol is made from sugar and flour. When a person overeats sweets, flour products, and carbohydrates; such as, beans, bread, and potatoes, his body becomes an alcohol factory and he is literally intoxicating himself daily as fermentation takes place. The effect of all these toxic poisons hinders normal body functions, clouds the mind and the senses, and grieves the Holy Spirit.

Gluttony is eating too much and causes Christians to become carnal: that is, spiritually insensitive, lazy, having unnatural desires for sex, and a mind polluted with ungodly thoughts. Gluttony, of which many Christians are guilty, is sin. I've been to many church meetings where gluttony was a game! Some ate until they became sick. Others laughed and made fun of me because I would not join in their diabolical excess. Jesus has a word for this "Christian" nation. "And take heed to yourselves, lest any time your hearts be overcharged with surfeiting, [overeating] and drunkenness, and cares of this life, and so that day come upon you unawares. For as a snare shall it come on all them who dwell on the face of the whole earth. Watch ye therefore, and pray always, that ye may be accounted worthy to escape all these things that shall come to pass, and to stand before the Son of man" (Luke 21:34-36, AKJV).

Is it any wonder that pastors have no power to speak out and stand against the beer and liquor distributors, drunkenness, and horrible alcoholic traffic of this nation, when they themselves are gluttons, enslaved to their own bellies! My observation across this nation is that even in so-called Bible-believing churches, Sunday has become a feast day instead of a fast day. If a big meal is served, it is usually on Sunday just after the sermon! So instead of going away from the service and meditating on the Word of God to put it to practice, they immediately stuff themselves with greasy food until they are groggy and fall asleep under the influence of the toxins produced in their bodies, sinking deeper into their gluttony, carnality, and their god (Phil 3:19).

Once a person has been on a long fast and has cleansed himself of many bad physical and mental habits that he may yield more fully unto the Lord, and present his body holy and acceptable unto the Lord, he will want to fast regularly and pray that the power of darkness be broken in homes across his nation (Eph. 6:10-18).

—Becoming Drug Free

The quickest and surest way to break any drug habit is by prayer and fasting. The Christian has been given the most powerful armor in this respect. Whether the drugs be nicotine, coffee, tea, alcohol, marijuana, heroine, cocaine, crack cocaine, methadone, fasting cleanses the body of these and takes away forever the natural desire for them. How long one will have to fast and pray will depend upon how long one has been a slave to these drugs.

I've talked to some Christians who would rather be bound by their cigarettes the rest of their lives than to go on a three-day fast and be free of them forever and be used of God with a clean testimony. What are a few days of headaches and withdrawal symptoms in comparison to a fruitful life for the Lord Jesus? With what shame many Christians will hope to go into heaven and spend all eternity with their Lord and Redeemer, Jesus, when they refuse to suffer a few days here on earth to bear a good testimony before many witnesses.

—Breaking Free as a Result of Fasting

Prayer and fasting will bring glorious liberty to prayer in the Spirit and faith to believe God for every one of His numerous promises in His Holy Word. If you start a chain of praying folks in your fellowship, God will begin to heal the sick and save souls, because it is written: "...for as soon as Zion [the church] travailed, she brought forth her children" (Isa. 66:8, AKJV). Prayer with fasting will increase the burden for the salvation of souls. Every man of God who holds large salvation and healing campaigns has fasted at least two or three weeks preceding the meetings. Some of them eat nothing during the entire time of the crusade.

Prayer and fasting act as a refining fire and burn out the bad thoughts—criticism, envy, and hatred—allowing you to be filled with love and compassion for the lost. The Holy Spirit helps you love everyone in spite of their faults, their beliefs or even what they say or don't say. The Holy Spirit gives you a desire to forgive all and to love even your enemies. "Dear friends, we must love each other because love comes from God. Everyone who loves has been born from God and knows God. The person who doesn't love doesn't know God, because God is love. God has shown us his love by sending his only Son into the world so that we could have life through him. This is love: not that we have loved God, but that he loved us and sent his Son to be the payment for our sins" (1 John 4:7-10, GW). " We love because God loved us first. Whoever says, 'I love God,' but hates another believer is a liar. People who don't love other believers, whom they have seen, can't love God, whom they have not seen. Christ has given us this commandment: The person who loves God must also love other believers" (1 John 4:19-21, GW). This is the true representation of the cross.

Through prayer and fasting the Holy Spirit renews your mind and reveals the Word of God to you in a way that you can never imagine. David said, "Search me, God, and know my heart; test me and know my concerns.

See if there is any offensive way in me; lead me in the everlasting way" (Psalm 139:23-24, HCSB).

By being continually filled and led by the Holy Spirit you will see more clearly that all of those who love Jesus and are washed in His blood are members of His Body, which is the Church. And His body has one and only one head, the Lord Jesus Christ Himself. He will give you an unprejudiced love for every member of His body, no matter what country, race, or social strata they come from.

When a person gives himself to prayer and fasting with the sole purpose of looking into the face of the Lord Jesus Christ moment by moment, the Holy Spirit will transform him from glory to glory, light to light, revelation to revelation, victory to victory, into the same image of Jesus Himself. "We all, with unveiled faces, are reflecting the glory of the Lord and are being transformed into the same image from glory to glory; this is from the Lord who is the Spirit" (2 Cor 3:18, HCSB).

CHAPTER EIGHT

PAST AND PRESENT FASTING ACCOUNTS

Every great Christian leader who has moved his generation mightily for God was one who fasted.

The first gleam of real spiritual reformation that appeared after the night of the Dark Ages occurred in the 14th century under the preaching of Savonarola in Florence, Italy. In response to this flaming preacher, almost all Florence professed conversion to Christ for a period of time. This great preacher was an one who fasted regularly. Historians state that he often could keep his place in the pulpit with difficulty, so weak was he from abstaining from food. His spiritual movement became so menacing to the papacy that the church authorities turned on him and finally burned him at the stake in the plaza of the city where his mighty triumphs had taken place.

As the fires that took the life of this tremendous preacher

were lighting the skies in Florence, the divine plans were approaching consummation in Germany for the birth of the great reformation led by Martin Luther. Of this bold and faithful Christian it is said that he fasted consistently. Consider the results! The tremendous religious and spiritual change that was wrought in Europe and America by the activities of this man, now enables us to have the great privilege of knowing our magnificent Savior. So now it is our turn to prepare for the next generation. In this case, prayer and fasting enabled God to do what otherwise He was unable to do. And powerful forces for good were released that brought many thousands out of the superstition and bondage of Romanism, into a knowledge of the born-again experience. This revival ran like a flame in the later years in the colonial portions of America. Fasting was an important part of this great awakening.

Contemporary with Martin Luther and the great reformation that brought thousands of people out of the bondage of Romanism, was a group of noted religious reformers, each one leading a wing of the amazing spiritual renaissance. It is very convicting to learn how universally the principles of prayer and fasting characterized these leaders, and brought to each the most remarkable victory.

John Calvin, in Geneva, was an inveterate prayer warrior who fasted, and lived to see his prayers answered in the conversion of almost a whole city. It is stated that there was not one house in the city of Geneva that did not have at least one praying person in it.

John Knox, in Scotland, fasted and waited on God until intervening providence drove Mary Queen of Scots into exile in England and finally to the block. A familiar quotation representing the queen declared that she feared "John Knox and his prayers more than the armies of Elizabeth, Queen of England." Knox fasted regularly. The leaders of the reformation in England, some of them paying with martyrdom for their part in it, were said to practice fasting as faithfully as they offered prayers. Latimer, Ridley, and Cranmer, all martyred for their convictions, were among this group.

John Wesley laid great importance to this spiritual exercise by following the spiritual custom of fasting twice a week, Wednesday and Friday, until 4 p.m. He is understood to have said that he would as soon think of cursing and swearing as to omit the weekly custom of fasting. And look at the amazing religious movement that the Holy Spirit brought through His instrument! The early Methodists in America practiced fasting faithfully, and church history records the amazing revival victories that characterized the spread of the followers of John Wesley in this country. It is also noted that John Wesley would not ordain a minister unless that person fasted. The people who constituted the early holiness movement also fasted faithfully and the sanctified life was supposed to include some fasting every week.

Jonathan Edwards, of New England, was a colossal colonial figure. He launched a far-reaching and influential revival in those early days. He is said to have fasted and prayed until he was too weak to stand in the pulpit, but how wonderfully God ministered through him!

Charles G. Finney was a confirmed believer in this heaven-blessed exercise. He declares that when he detected a diminution of the Spirit's wonderful presence in and through him, he would fast for three days and nights. He bears testimony that as a result he was invariably again filled with the marvelous power that caused thousands of professional men, leading society women, merchants, and well-to-do, as well as hundreds of thousands of the common people, to break down with conviction and yield to God for salvation. Finney believed strongly in biblical fasting as one of the means of releasing God's amazing power.

—FASTING TODAY

Every Christian should pray and fast in accordance with God's Word. No one is too old to pray and fast. It is not necessary to understand all of the details of a spiritual truth to obey God in that truth. I do not understand all about prayer, but I pray and reap the benefit of the spiritual promises. Neither do I understand everything about fasting, but I fast and reap the benefit of that promise also. Under the Old Covenant, Israel was required by God to fast collectively at least once a year on the Day of Atonement, and on other occasions, too, like the Prophet Samuel at Mizhpa. There are also records of individuals who fasted: Moses, David, Elijah, and many of the kings of Israel led their people in fasting. In the book of Acts, we have records of the early church fasting together in groups for special needs., particularly when they where sending forth apostles and appointing leaders in the local churches. In accordance with God's Word, the Apostle Paul makes a distinction between being hungry (being forced to suffer for Jesus for lack of food), and fasting. "I have lived with weariness and pain and sleepless nights. Often I have been hungry and thirsty and have gone without food; often I have shivered with cold, without enough clothing to keep me warm" (2 Cor. 11:27, TLB).

In fasting often. Paul saw fasting as a way of ministering unto the Lord. One of the main purposes for which every Christian should pray and fast is to receive faith to believe God for the fulfillment of His promises.

"About that time King Herod moved against some of the believers, and killed the apostle James (John's brother). When Herod saw how much this pleased the Jewish leaders, he arrested Peter during the Passover celebration and imprisoned him, placing him under the guard of sixteen soldiers. Herod's intention was to deliver Peter to the Jews for execution after the Passover. But earnest prayer was going up to God from the church for his safety all the time he was in prison.

"The night before he was to be executed, he was asleep, double-chained between two soldiers with others standing guard before the prison gate, when suddenly there was a light in the cell and an angel of the Lord stood beside Peter! The angel slapped him on the side to awaken him and said, 'Quick! Get up!' And the chains fell off his wrists! Then the angel told him, 'Get dressed and put on your shoes.' And he did. 'Now put on your coat and follow me!' the angel ordered.

"So Peter left the cell, following the angel. But all the time he thought it was a dream or vision and didn't believe it was really happening" (Acts 12:1-9, TLB).

CHAPTER NINE

CONCLUSION

We have covered many of the principle aspects of prayer and fasting. We defined prayer as the vehicle of communication with our Father based on Jeremiah 33:3, and fasting as abstaining from food for spiritual purposes. We saw fasting as the revealed will of God and that He has promised to reward those who diligently seek Him through the scriptural way of fasting based on Isaiah 58.

Jesus said: "If any man will come after me, let him deny himself, and take up his cross daily, and follow Me" (Luke 9:23, 24, AKJV). This is a plain call to mortify (put to death) the deeds of the flesh, that Christ may live His life in you. What you feed grows. If you feed the old-man nature, he will grow and dominate your life; if you by the Spirit put to death the deeds of the body and feed your Spirit on the living Word of God, you shall live.

Fasting is a vital spiritual exercise that puts to death the old-man nature and makes the way for Jesus to live His life in you.

The Apostle Paul said: "But I keep under my body, and bring it into subjection; lest that by any means, when I have preached to others, I myself should be a castaway" (1 Cor. 9:27, AKJV). One of the ways Paul pummeled his body and brought it into subjection was by prayer and fasting. In fastings often (2 Cor. 11:27). Instead of using the excuse that Christ did it all and refusing to fast and pray, can you say with Paul: "...I am made a minister; Who now rejoice in my sufferings for you, and fill up that which is behind of the afflictions of Christ in my flesh for His body's sake, which is the church..." (Col. 1:23-24, AKJV).

If the need was great to place such a burden on Paul in the first century, who dares to say that the need is not ten thousands times greater in this twenty-first century. The Spirit of God is crying out as in the days of old. "I looked for someone to stand up for me against all this, to repair the defenses of the city, to take a stand for me and stand in the gap to protect this land so I wouldn't have to destroy it. I couldn't find anyone. Not one" (Ezek 22:30, MSG).

God is looking for men and women to stand in the gap, to stem the tide of atheism, spiritualism, materialism, drugs, alcohol, false cults, wickedness and violence. In that day, will you be able to give an account for your witness to this generation? Will you be able to stand before His throne and say: "I was not ashamed?" (Rom. 1:16).

You can begin by prayer and fasting and deep heart-searching. You can call the armies of God together by word and by example and cry: "Sanctify ye a fast, call a solemn assembly, gather the elders and all the inhabitants of the land into the house of the Lord your God, and cry unto the Lord, Alas for the day! for the day of the Lord is at hand, and as a destruction from the Almighty shall it come" (Joel 1:14-15, AKJV).

You do not have to stand back and watch your home, your children, your nation be destroyed by the enemy. God has the answer: "If my people who are called by my name shall humble themselves, and pray and seek my face, and turn from their wicked ways, then I will hear from heaven, and will forgive their sin and heal their land" (2 Chron. 7:14).

JESUS CHRIST IS THE SAME YESTERDAY, TODAY AND FOREVER. (Heb.13:8) Call on Him and He will answer. It's a promise.

PRAYERS OF THE BIBLE

Subject	Reference

— ∼ —

Abijah's army—for victory	2 Chr. 13:15
Abraham—for a son	Gen. 15:1–6
Abraham—for Ishmael	Gen. 17:18–21
Abraham—for Sodom	Gen. 18:20–33
Abraham—for Abimelech	Gen. 20:17
Abraham's servant—for guidance	Gen. 24:12–52
Asa—for victory	2 Chr. 14:11

— ∼ —

Cain—for mercy	Gen. 4:13–15
Centurion—for his servant	Matt. 8:5–13
Christians—for Peter	Acts 12:5–12
Christians—for kings in authority	1 Tim. 2:1, 2
Corinthians—for Paul	2 Cor. 1:9–11
Cornelius—for enlightenment	Acts 10:1–33
Criminal—for salvation	Luke 23:42, 43

— ∼ —

Daniel—for the Jews	Dan. 9:3–19
Daniel—for knowledge	Dan. 2:17–23
David—for blessing	2 Sam. 7:18–29
David—for help	1 Sam. 23:10–13
David—for guidance	2 Sam. 2:1
David—for grace	Ps. 25:16
David—for justice	Ps. 9:17–20
Disciples—for boldness	Acts 4:24–31

— ∼ —

Elijah—for drought and rain	James 5:17, 18
Elijah—for the raising the widow's son to life	1 Kings 17:20–23
Elijah—for triumph over Baal	1 Kings 18:36–38
Elijah—for death	1 Kings 19:4
Elisha—for blindness and sight	2 Kings 6:17–23
Ezekiel—for undefilement	Ezek. 4:12–15
Ezra—for the sins of the people	Ezra 9:6–15

— ∼ —

Gideon—for proof of his call	Judg. 6:36–40

— ∼ —

Habakkuk—for deliverance	Hab. 3:1–19
Habakkuk—for justice	Hab. 1:1–4

Hagar—for consolation	Gen. 21:14–20
Hannah—for a son	1 Sam. 1:10–17
Hezekiah—for deliverance	2 Kings 19:15–19
Hezekiah—for health	2 Kings 20:1–11
Holy Spirit—for Christians	Rom. 8:26, 27

— ∼ —

Isaac—for children	Gen. 25:21, 24–26
Israelites—for deliverance	Ex. 2:23–25; 3:7–10

— ∼ —

Jabez—for prosperity	1 Chr. 4:10
Jacob—all night	Gen. 32:24–30
Jacob—for deliverance from Esau	Gen. 32:9–12
Jehoahaz—for victory	2 Kings 13:1–5
Jehoshaphat—for protection	2 Chr. 20:5–12, 27
Jehoshaphat—for victory	2 Chr. 18:31
Jeremiah—for Judah	Jer. 42:1–6
Jeremiah—for mercy	Jer. 14:7–10
Jesus—Lord's Prayer	Matt. 6:9–13
Jesus—praise for revelation to babes	Matt. 11:25, 26
Jesus—at Lazarus's tomb	John 11:41, 42
Jesus—for the Father's glory	John 12:28
Jesus—for the Church	John 17:1–26
Jesus—for deliverance	Matt. 26:39, 42, 44; 27:46
Jesus—for forgiveness for others	Luke 23:34
Jesus—in submission	Luke 23:46
Jews—for safe journey	Ezra 8:21, 23
Jonah—for deliverance from the fish	Jonah 2:1–10
Joshua—for help and mercy	Josh. 7:6–9

— ∼ —

Leper—for healing	Matt. 8:2, 3

— ∼ —

Manasseh—for deliverance	2 Chr. 33:12, 13
Manoah—for guidance	Judg. 13:8–15
Moses—for Pharaoh	Ex. 8:9–13
Moses—for water	Ex. 15:24, 25
Moses—for Israel	Ex. 32:31–35
Moses—for Miriam	Num. 12:11–14
Moses—that he might see the Promised Land	Dt. 3:23–25; 34:1–4
Moses—for a successor	Num. 27:15–17

— ∼ —

Nehemiah—for the Jews   Neh. 1:4–11

— ∼ —

Paul—for the healing of Publius's father   Acts 28:8
Paul—for the Ephesians   Eph. 3:14–21
Paul—for grace   2 Cor. 12:8, 9
People of Judah—for a covenant   2 Chr. 15:12–15
Peter—for the raising of Dorcas   Acts 9:40
Priests—for blessing   2 Chr. 30:27

— ∼ —

Rebekah—for understanding   Gen. 25:22, 23
Reubenites—for victory   1 Chr. 5:18–20

— ∼ —

Samson—for water   Judg. 15:18, 19
Samson—for strength   Judg. 16:29, 30
Samuel—for Israel   1 Sam. 7:5–12
Solomon—for wisdom   1 Kings 3:6–14

— ∼ —

Tax collector—for mercy   Luke 18:13

— ∼ —

Zechariah—for a son   Luke 1:13

FASTING IN THE BIBLE

A

Ahab   1 Kings 21:4,5; 21:27
An Egyptian Servant of an Amalekite   1 Sam. 30:12
Anna   Luke 2:37

C

Cornelius   Acts 10:30, 31
Crew and Passengers on the Ship of   Acts 27:33
Adramyttium

D

Daniel   Dan. 9:3; 10:2, 3
Darius   Dan. 6:18; Ps. 35:13;
David   Ps. 69:10;
     2 Sam. 3:35;

	12:15-17; Ps. 109:24
Disciples of John The Baptist	Matt. 9:14; Mk 2:18;
	Luke 5:33

E

Elijah	1 Kings 19:8
Esther	Esther 4:15, 16
Ezra	Ezra 9:5; 10:6

H

Hannah	1 Sam. 1:7, 8

I

Israel, Before the Battle Against Benjamin	Judges 20:26
Israel, at Mizpah	1 Sam. 7:6

J

Jesus	Matt. 4:1, 2;
	Luke 4:1,2 2
Jews Committed to Killing Paul	Acts 23:12, 13
Jews During the reign of Ahasuerus	Esther 4:3; 4:15, 16
John The Baptist	Matt. 11:18;
	Luke 7:33
Jonathan	1 Sam. 20:34
Judah, and Jehoshaphat feared	2 Chr. 20:3, 4

L

Leaders of The Church at Antioch	Acts 13:1-3

M

Men of Jabesh Gilead	1 Sam 31:11-13;
	1 Chr. 10:11, 12
Mighty Men of David	2 Sam. 1:12
Moses	Ex. 34:28;
	Dt. 9:9; 9:18
Multitudes Following Jesus	Matt. 15:32;
	Mark 8:2, 3

N

Nehemiah	Neh 1:4

P

Paul	Acts 9:9; 2 Cor. 6:5, 11:27
People of Judah during the reign of Jehoiakim	Jer. 36:9, 10
People of Nineveh	Jonah 3:5-9
Pharisees	Matt. 9:14; Mk. 2:18; Luke 5:33

R

Remnant in Jerusalem After the Captivity	Neh. 9:1
Remnant Returning After the Captivity	Ezra 8:21-23

S

Saul	1 Sam. 28:20
Saul's, Army	1 Sam. 14:24

U

Uriah	2 Sam. 11:11

NAMES, TITLES & ATTRIBUTES OF GOD

"Because he is lovingly devoted to Me, I will deliver him; I will exalt him because he knows My name" (Psalm 91:14, HCSB).

"Those who know Your name trust in You because You have not abandoned those who seek You, LORD" (Psalm 9:10, HCSB).

Meditate on the Name of God while ministering to Him.

A

Abounding in goodness and truth	Ex. 34:6
Acquainted with grief	Isa. 53:3
Adam, the Last	1 Cor. 15:45
Advocate with the Father	1 John 2:1
ALL	Col. 3:11

Almighty, the	Job 5:17, 1:8
Alpha	Rev. 1:8, 21:6
Altogether lovely	Song of Sol. 5:16
Amen, the	Rev. 3:14
Ancient of Days, the	Dan. 7:22
Anointed	Ps. 2:2, Acts 4:27
Apostle and High Priest of our confession	Heb. 3:1
Author and finisher of our faith, the	Heb. 12:2
Author of eternal salvation, the	Heb. 5:9

B

Banner to the people	Isa. 11:10
Beginning of the creation of God	Rev. 3:14
Beginning	Rev. 21:6
Beloved	Matt. 12:18
Branch of the Lord	Isa. 4:2
Branch	Isa. 11:1
Branch, a righteous	Jer. 23:5
Branch	Zech. 6:12
Bread from heaven, true	John 6:32
Bread of Life	John 6:35
Breath of the Almighty	Job 32:8, 33:4
Bridegroom	Matt. 9:15
Brightness of His glory	Heb. 1:3
Brother of James, Joses, Judas, and Simon	Mark 6:3
Builder and Maker	Heb. 11:10

C

Carpenter	Mark 6:3
Carpenter's Son	Matt. 13:55
Chief Cornerstone, Elect, Precious	1 Pet. 2:6
Chief Cornerstone	Matt. 21:42; Mark 12:10; Eph. 2:20
Child Jesus	Luke 2:37
Chosen of God, the	Luke 23:35
Christ, the chosen of God	Luke 23:35
Christ Jesus My Lord	Phil. 3:8
Christ of God	Luke 9:20
Christ, the	Matt. 16: 6
Comforter	2 Cor. 1:4

Commander of the Lord's army, the	Josh. 5:15
Confidence of all the end of the earth	Ps. 65:5
Consolation of Israel	Luke 2:25
Cornerstone, and Precious	Isa. 28:16
Counselor, Wonderful	Isa. 9:6
Covenant to the people	Isa. 42: 6
Creator of Israel	Isa. 43:15
Creator of the end of the earth	Isa. 40:28
Creator, a Faithful	1 Pet. 4:19
Creator, Your	Eccl. 12:1
Crown of glory, a	Isa. 28:5, 62:3

D

Dayspring, the	Luke 1:78
Defender of widows	Ps. 68:5
Deliverer	2 Sam. 22:2; Ps. 18:2
Deliverer, the	Rom. 11:26
Desire of all nations	Hag. 2:7
Diadem of beauty	Isa. 28:5
Diadem of royal	Isa. 62:3
Door of the sheep	John 10: 7
Door, the	John 10:9
Dwelling place	Ps. 90:1
Dwelling, your	Ps. 91:9

E

End, the	Rev. 21:6
Excellent Glory	2 Pet. 1:17
Express Image of His Person	Heb. 1: 3
Everlasting strength	Isa. 26: 4

F

Faithful and truth	Rev. 19:11
Father	Matt. 11: 25
Father of Glory	Eph. 1:17
Father of lights	James 1:17
Father of Mercies	2 Cor. 2:13
Father of Spirits	Heb. 12:9
Father of the fatherless	Ps. 68:5
Father of Israel	Jer. 31:9
Father who Honors Me	John 8:54

Father, Everlasting	Isa. 9:6
Father, Holy	John 17:11, 20:17
Father, My	John 8:54
Father, our	Isa. 64:8
Father, righteous	John 17:25
Father, your	Deut. 32:6;
	John 20:17
Fear of Isaac	Gen. 31:42
Fire, a consuming	Deut. 4:24
Fire, the devouring	Isa. 33:14
First to rise from the dead	Acts 26:33
First, the	Isa. 44:6; Rev. 22:13
Firstborn among many brethren	Rom. 8:29
First fruit of those who have fallen as sleep	1 Cor. 15:20
For a trap and a snare	Isa. 8:14
Fortress, my	Ps. 18:2; 91:2
Foundation	1 Cor. 3:11
Foundation, or sure	Isa. 28:16
Fountain of living waters, the	Jer. 2:13
Friends of tax collectors and sinners	Matt. 11:19

G

Gift, indescribable	2 Cor. 9:15
Gift, the same	Acts 11:17
Glory, their	Ps. 106:20; Jer. 2: 11
Glory, your	Isa. 60:19
God	Gen. 1:1; John 1:1
God of Host El Sabaoth	Ps. 80:7
God of my Salvation	Ps. 18:46
God of your Salvation	Isa. 17:10
God and Father or our Lord Jesus Christ	Eph. 1:3
God and Savior Jesus Christ	2 Pet. 1:1
God and Savior, our great	Titus 2:13
God in Heaven above and our earth beneath	Dt. 4:39; Josh. 2:11
God in Heaven that revealeth secrets	Dan. 2:28
God Most High, El Elyon	Gen. 14:18
God my Maker	Job 35:10
God my Rock	Ps. 42:9
God of Abraham	Ps. 47:9
God of Abraham Isaac and Jacob	1 Kings 18:36
God of all comfort	2 Cor. 1:3

God of all grace	1 Pet. 5:10
God of all flesh	Jer. 32:27
God of all kingdom of the earth	2 Kings 19:15
God of Daniel	Dan. 6:26
God of David your father	2 Kings 20:5
God of glory	Ps. 29:3
God of gods	Dt. 10:17
God of heaven	Gen. 24:3; Ps. 136:26
God of heaven and earth	Ezra 5:11
God of Israel	Ex. 24:10;
	Matt. 15:31
God of Jacob	Ps. 20:1; 46:7
God of Jeshurun (Israel) The upright one	Dt. 33:26
God of mercy	Ps. 59:10
God of my father Abraham	Gen. 32:9
God of my salvation	Ps. 51:14, 88:1
God of my strength	Ps. 43:2
God of Nahor	Gen. 31:53
God or our fathers	Dt. 26:7
God of our Lord Jesus Christ	Eph. 1:17
God of our salvation	1 Chr. 16:35; Ps. 85:4
God of peace	Rom. 16:20;
	1 Thess. 5:23
God or recompense	Jer. 51:56
God of Shadrach, Meshach and Abednego	Dan. 3:28
God of the armies of Israel	Isa. 17:45
God of the earth	Gen. 24:3
God of the Hebrews	Ex. 5:3
God of the living	Matt. 22:32
God of the spirit of all flesh	Num. 16:22, 27:15
God of the whole earth	Isa. 54:5
God of truth	Ps. 31:5
God of truth without injustice	Dt. 32:4
God of your fathers	Dt. 1:21
God our father	Eph. 1:2
God our Savior	Jude 25
God our strength	Ps. 81:1
God over Israel	2 Sam. 7:26
God the father	John 6:27
God the king of all the earth	Ps. 47:7
God the Lord	1 Chr. 13:6; Ps. 85:8

God who alone is wise	1 Tim. 1:17
God who avenges me	Ps. 18:47
God who does wonders	Ps. 77:14
God who forgives	Ps. 99:8
God who delivers me from my enemies	Ps. 18:47-48
God who sees	Gen. 16:13
God, a jealous	Dt. 4:24
God, Almighty El Shaddai	Gen. 17:1
God, Great and Awesome	Dan. 9:4
God, Israel	1 Chr. 17: 24
God, living	Jer. 10:10
God, living and true	1 Thess. 1:9
God, merciful and gracious	Ex. 34:6
God, mighty	Isa. 9:6
God, my	Gen. 28:21;
	John 20:17
God of my righteousness Jehovah Tsidkenu	Ps. 4:1
God of King	Ps. 145:1
God, the Everlasting	Gen. 21:33; Isa. 40:28
God, the faithful	Dt. 7:9
God, Great	Dt. 10:17
God, the great and awesome	Neh. 1:5
God, the true	Jer. 10:10
God, your	John 20:17
Guarantee	2 Cor. 1:22, 5:5
Guide, our	Ps. 48:14

H

Habitation of justice	Jer. 50:7
He who blots out our transgressions	Isa. 43:25
He who built all things	Heb. 3:4
He who calls for the water of the sea	Amos 5:8
He who comes in the name of the Lord	Ps. 118:26
He who comforts you	Isa. 51:12
He who declares to man what is thought is	Amos 4:13
He who raised Christ from the dead	Rom. 8:11
He who reveals secrets	Dan. 2:29
He who sanctifies	Heb. 2:11
He who searches the hearts	Rom. 8:27
He who searches the minds and hearts	Rev. 2:23
He who from the shadow of death In the morning	Amos 5:8

He who was dead and came to life	Rev. 2:8
Head of all principality and power	Col. 2:10
Head of the body, the church	Col. 1:18
Head of the church	Eph. 5:23
Heir of all things	Heb. 1:2
Help in trouble a very present help	Ps. 46:1
Help, my	Ps. 27:9, 40:17
Help, our	Ps. 33:20
Helper of the fatherless, the	Ps. 10:14
Helper, another	John 14:16
Helper, the	John 14:26
He who was the seven spirits of God	Rev. 3:1
He who lives	Rev. 1:8
Hiding place, my	Ps. 32:7
High Priest forever	Heb. 6:20
High Priest over the house of God	Heb. 10:21
High Priest, a great	Heb. 4:14
High Priest, a merciful and faithful	Heb. 2:17
Him who is able to keep you from stumbling	Jude 24
Him who is able to present you faultless	Jude 24
Him who is from the beginning	1 John 2:13
Him who is must just	Job 34:17
Him who is ready to judge the living and dead	1 Pet. 4:5
Him who lives forever	Dan. 12:7
Him who lives forever and ever	Rev. 10:6
Him who loved us and washed us From our sins	Rev. 1:5-6
Him who ought to be feared	Ps. 76:11
Him who sits on the throne	Rev. 5:13
Holy one	Luke 1:35; 1 John 2:20; Isa. 43:15
Holy one and the Just	Acts 3:14
Holy one of God	Luke 4:34
Holy one of Israel	Ps. 71:22; Isa. 41:14
Holy one who is faithful	Hos. 11:12
Holy servant Jesus	Acts 4:27
Holy Spirit	John 14:26; Ps. 51: 11
Holy Spirit of God	Eph. 4:30
Holy Spirit, His	Isa. 63: 10
Holy Spirit, the promise of the	Acts 2: 33

Hope in the day of doom	Jer. 17:17
Hope of Israel, the	Jer. 14: 8
Hope of Israel, the	Jer. 17:13; Acts 28: 20
Hope of the Fathers	Jer. 50:7
Hope, my	Ps. 71:5
Horn of my Salvation	2 Sam. 22:3; Ps. 18:2
Horn of salvation	Luke 1: 69
Husband, my	Hos. 2:16
Husband, your	Isa. 54:5

I

I AM	Ex. 3:14; Job 8:58
I AM WHO I AM	Ex. 3:14
Image of God, the	2 Cor. 4:4
Image of the invisible God	Col. 1:15
Immanuel (God with us)	Matt. 1:23
Immortal	1 Tim. 1:17
Inheritance, their	Ezek. 44:28
Intercessor, my	Isa. 53:12
Invisible	1 Tim. 1:17

J

Jealous	Ex. 34:14
Jesus	Matt. 1: 21
Jesus Christ	John 1:17; Acts 2: 38
Jesus Christ of Nazareth	Acts 4:16
Judge of all the earth	Gen. 18:25
Judge of the earth	Ps. 94:2
Judge of the living and the dead	Acts 10:42
Judge, just	Ps. 7:11
Judge, our	Isa. 33:22
Judge, righteous, the	2 Tim. 4:8
Judge, the	Judges 11:27
Just One, the	Acts 7:52

K

King above all gods, the great	Ps. 95:3
King from of old, my	Ps. 74:12
King of all the earth, the	Ps. 47:7
King of glory, the	Ps. 24:7
King of heaven, the	Dan. 4:37

King of Israel, the	Zeph. 3:15; John 1:49
KING OF KINGS	Rev. 19:16
King of kings	1 Tim. 6:15
King of the Jews	Matt. 27: 11;
	John 18:39, 19:9
King of the nations	Jer. 10: 7
King of the saints	Rev. 15: 3
King over all the earth, the great	Ps. 47: 2
King who come in the name of the Lord	Luke 19:38
King everlasting	Jer. 10:10
King, great	Ps. 48: 2; Matt. 5: 35
King, my	Ps. 44: 4
King, our	Isa. 33: 22
King, your	Matt. 21:5; Isa. 43:15

L

Lamb of God, the	John 1:29
Lamb without blemish and without spot, a	1 Pet. 1:19
Lamb, a	Rev. 5:6
Lamb, the	Rev. 5:8
Lamb who was slain	Rev. 5:12
Lamp, my	2 Sam. 22:29
Last, the	Isa. 44:6; Rev. 22:13
Lawgiver, one	James 4:12
Law giver, our	Isa. 33:22
Leader and commander for the people, a	Isa. 55:4
Life, eternal	1 John 5:20
Life, our	Col. 3:4
Life, the	John 14:6
Light	1 John 1:5
Light, the true	John 1:8
Light of life, the	John 8:12
Light of men, the	John 1:14
Light of the world, the	John 8:12
Light to bring revelation to the gentiles	Luke 2:32
Light to the gentiles	Isa. 42:6
Light, a great	Isa. 9:2
Light, or everlasting	Isa. 60:19
Light, true	John 1:19
Lily of the valleys, the	Song of Sol. 2:1
Lion of the tribe of Judah	Rev. 5:5

Long suffering, the	Ex. 34:6
Lord	Luke 2:11
Lord Adonai	Ps. 54:4
Lord Jehovah	Gen. 15: 6
Lord and Savior, the	2 Pet. 3:2
Lord and Savior Jesus-Christ, the	2 Pet. 2:20
Lord God	Gen. 2:4
Lord God Almighty	Rev. 15:3
Lord God of gods, the	Josh. 22:22
Lord God of Hosts, the	2 Sam. 5:10
Lord God of Israel	1 Chr. 29:10
Lord God, the only	Jude 4
Lord is My Banner, the	Ex. 17:15; Num. 2:2
Lord is Peace "Jehovah-Shalom"	Judges 6:24
Lord Jesus	Luke 24:3; Acts 7:59
Lord Jesus-Christ our Hope	1 Tim. 1:1
Lord Most High	Ps. 7:17
Lord my rock	Ps. 28:1
Lord of all the earth, the	Josh. 3:13
Lord of both the dead and the living	Rom. 14:9
Lord of Glory, the	James 2:1; 1 Cor. 2:8
Lord of heaven and earth	Matt. 11:25
Lord of Hosts	Ps. 24:10
Lord of Kings	Dan. 2:47
Lord of Lords	Rev. 19:16
Lord of lords	Dt. 10:17; 1 Tim. 6:15; Rev. 17:14
Lord of Peace, the	2 Thess. 3:16
Lord of the harvest	Matt. 9:38
Lord of the Sabbath	Matt. 12:8; Luke 6:5
Lord our God, the	Josh. 24:24
Lord our Maker, the	Ps. 95:6
Lord our righteousness, the	Jer. 23:6, 33:16
Lord our shield	Ps. 59:11
Lord over Israel	1 Chr. 28:5
Lord who heals you, the	Ex. 15:26
Lord who made heaven and earth	Ps. 115:15, 121:2
Lord who sanctifies you, the	Ex. 31:13
Lord will provide, the	Gen. 22:14
Lord your God, the	Lev. 11:44

Lord your maker, the	Isa. 51:13
Lord, my	John 20:28
Love	1 John 4:8

M

Maker of all things, the	Jer. 10:16
Maker of heaven and earth the sea, and	Ps. 146:6
Maker of the bear, Orion, and the Pleiades	Job 9:9
Majestic Lord, the	Isa. 33:21
Majesty on high, the	Heb. 1:3
Maker, His	Prov. 14:31
Maker, My	Job 32:22
Maker, our	Ps. 95:6
Maker, your	Isa. 54:5
Man attested by God	Acts 2:22
Man Jesus-Christ, the	1 Tim. 2:5
Man of sorrows	Isa. 53:3
Man, a righteous	Luke 23:47
Man, the second	1 Cor. 15:47
Man, that just	Matt. 29:19
Man, the	John 19:5
Man, this	Mark 6:2
Master	Luke 5:5; 2 Tim. 2:21
Master in heaven, a	Col. 4:1
Mediator, the	1 Tim. 2:5
Mediator of the New Covenant	Mal. 3:1
Mighty one of Jacob, the	Ps. 132:2-5; Act 7:46
Mighty God	Isa. 9:6
Mighty God of Jacob	Gen. 49:24
Messiah, the	John 1:41
Morning star	2 Pet. 1:19
Morning star, the bright and	Rev. 22:16
Most High	Ps. 18:13, 92:1
Most high over all the earth, the	Ps. 83:18
Most Holy, the	Dan. 9:24
Most upright	Isa. 26:2

N

Nazarene, a	Matt. 2:23

O

Offering and sacrifice to God, an	Eph. 5:2

Oil of gladness	Heb. 1:9
Omega	Rev. 1:8
Only begotten of the father	John 1:14
One greater than Solomon	Matt. 12:42
One greater than the temple	Matt. 12:6
One lawgiver who is able to save and destroy	James 4:12
One who gives salvation to kings	Ps. 144:10
One who is and who was and who is to be, the	Rev. 16:5
One who remembered us in our low state	Ps. 136:23
One you are to dread	Isa. 8:13
One you are to fear	Isa. 8:13
One you should hallow, the	Isa. 8:13
One, my elect	Isa. 42:1

P

Passover, our	1 Cor. 5:7
Peace, our	Eph. 2:14
Physician	Luke 4:23
Portion, my	Ps. 119:57
Portion in the land of the living	Ps. 142:5
Portion of Jacob, the	Jer. 10:16
Portion of my inheritance, the	Ps. 16:5
Possessor of heaven an earth	Gen. 14:22
Possession, their (Priests)	Isa. 44:28
Potentate, blessed and only	1 Tim. 6:15
Potter, the	Isa. 64:8; Rom. 9:21
Power of the highest	Luke 1:35
Power of God, the	1 Cor. 1:24
Power, the	Matt. 26:24
Praises of Israel, the	Ps. 22:3
Praise, your	Deut. 10:21
Priest forever according to The order of Melchizedek	Heb. 5:6
Prince, the	Dan. 9:25
Prince and savior	Acts 5:31
Prince of life	Acts 3:15
Prince of peace, the	Isa. 9:6
Prince of Princes, the	Dan. 8:25
Prince of host, the	Dan. 8:11
Promise, the father of	Acts 1:14
Prophet who is to come in the world	John 6:14
Prophet from Nazareth, the	Matt. 21:11

Prophet, the	John 7:40
Propitiation for our sins, the	1 John 2:2

R

Rabbi	John 3:2
Rabboni (teacher)	John 20:16
Ransom for all, a	1 Tim. 2:6
Redeemer from everlasting, our	Isa. 63:16
Redeemer, my	Job 19:25; Ps. 19:14
Redeemer, your	Isa. 41:14
Refiner and purifier, as a	Mal. 3:3
Refuge and strength, our	Ps. 46:1
Refuge for the oppressed	Ps. 9:9
Refuge, from the storm	Isa. 25:4
Refuge in the day of affliction, my	Jer. 16:19
Refuge in the day of trouble, my	Ps. 59:16
Refuge in times of trouble, a	Ps. 9:9
Refuge, my	2 Sam. 22:3; Ps. 145:5, 91:2
Refuge, our	Ps. 46:7
Refuge of his anointed, saving	Ps. 28:8
Resurrection and the life	John 11:25
Reward, you exceeding great	Gen. 15:1
Righteousness and sanctification and redemption, our	1 Cor. 1:20
Rock of his salvation	Deut. 32:15
Rock of my refuge, the	Ps. 94:22
Rock of my strength and my refuge, the	Ps. 62:7
Rock of offense, a	1 Pet. 2:8
Rock of our salvation, the	Ps. 95:1
Rock of Israel, the	2 Sam. 23:3
Rock, my	Ps. 18:3, 92:15
Rock, spiritual	1 Cor. 10:4
Rock, the	Deut. 32:4
Root and the offspring of David, the	Rev. 22:16
Root of David	Rev. 5:5
Root of Jesse	Isa. 11:10
Rose of Sharon, the	Song of Sol. 2:1
Ruler of the King of the earth	Rev. 1:5
Ruler, a (Governor)	Matt. 2:6

S

Salvation, my	Ex. 15:2; Ps. 27:1
Salvation, your	Luke 2:30
Sanctuary, a	Isa. 8:14
Savior in time of trouble (Israel)	Jer. 14:8
Savior Jesus	Acts 13:23
Savior of all men, the	1 Tim. 4:10
Savior of the body	Eph. 5:23
Savior of the world, the	John 4:24
Savior, my	2 Sam. 22:3
Savior, the	Eph. 5:23
Savior, their	Isa. 63:8
Savior, your	Isa. 43:3
Sceptre	Num. 24:17
Seal, a	Eph. 1:13
Seed, His	1 John 3:9
Seed, his (Abraham)	Gal. 3:16
Seed, the	Gal. 3:19
Servant to the circumcision	Rom. 15:8
Servant, Holy	Acts 4:27
Servant, my	Matt. 12:18
Servant, my righteous	Isa. 53:11
Seven spirits of God (the seven) the spirit	Rev. 5:6
Shade at your right hand, your	Ps. 121:5
Shade from the heart	Isa. 25:4
Shelter for his people, a	Joel 3:16
Shepherd and overseer of your souls, the	1 Pet. 2:25
Shepherd of Israel	Ps. 88:1
Shepherd of the sheep, great	Heb. 13:20
Shepherd one	Eccl. 12:11
Shepherd, the chief	1 Pet. 5:4
Shepherd, the good	John 10:11
Shield for me, a	Ps. 3:3
Shield, my	Ps. 18:2; 28:7
Shield, our	Ps. 33:20
Son of Abraham	Matt. 1:1
Son of David	Matt. 1:1; Luke 20:41
Son of God	John 1:49, 4:9
Son of Joseph	John 6:42
Son of Mary	Mark 6:3
Son of man, the	Matt. 12:40, 24:27

Son of the blessed one, the	Mark 14:61
Son of the living God	Matt. 16:16
Son of the most high God	Mark 5:7
Son, my beloved	Mark 1:11
Song, my	Ps. 118:14
Spirit of adoption, the	Rom. 8:15
Spirit of burning, the	Isa. 4:4
Spirit of Christ, the	Rom. 8:9
Spirit of counsel and might, the	Isa. 11:2
Spirit of faith, the	2 Cor. 4:13
Spirit of glory, the	1 Pet. 4:14
Spirit of God, the	Gen. 1:2; Matt. 3:16
Spirit of grace, the	Heb. 10:29
Spirit of grace and supplication, the	Zech. 12:10
Spirit of his son	Gal. 4:6
Spirit of holiness	Rom. 1:4
Spirit of Jesus-Christ, the	Phil. 1:19
Spirit of judgment, the	Isa. 4:4
Spirit of justice, a	Isa. 28:6
Spirit of knowledge and of the fear of the Lord	Isa. 11:2
Spirit of life, the	Rom. 8:2
Spirit of our God, the	1 Cor. 6:11
Spirit of the living God, the	2 Cor. 3:3
Spirit of the Lord, the	Isa. 11:2; Luke 4:18
Spirit of truth, the	John 14:17, 15:26
Spirit of wisdom and understanding, the	Isa. 11:2
Spirit of wisdom and revelation	Eph. 1:17
Spirit of your father, the	Matt. 10:20
Spirit of wisdom, the	Deut. 34:9
Spirit who bears witness, the	1 John 5:6
Spirit who dwells in us, the	James 4:5
Spirit, a life giving	1 Cor. 15:45
Spirit, a new	Ezek. 11:19, 18:31
Spirit, the eternal	Heb. 9:14
Spirit, his	Num. 11:29; Eph. 3:16
Spirit, my	Gen. 6:3; Matt. 12:18
Spirit, the	Num. 11:17; Acts 16:7
Spirit, your	Neh. 9:30
Spirit, your Good	Neh. 9:20

Star, a	Num. 24:17
Stone of stumbling	Isa. 8:14; 1 Pet. 2:8
Stone which the builders rejected	Matt. 21:42;
	Mark. 12:10;
	1 Pet. 2:7
Stone, a living	1 Pet. 2:4
Stone, a tried	Isa. 28:16
Stone of Israel, the	Gen. 49:24
Strength of my life	Ps. 27:1
Strength to the needy in his distress	Isa. 25:4
Strength to the poor, a	Isa. 25: 4
Strength of Israel, the	1 Sam. 15:29
Strength of my heart, the	Ps. 73:26
Strength, his	Ps. 59:9
Strength, my	Ps. 28:7, 118:14
Stronghold, my	Ps. 18:2
Sun and shield, a	Ps. 84:11
Support, my	2 Sam. 22:19;
	Ps. 18:18
Surety of a better covenant, a	Heb. 7:22
Sword of your majesty, the	Dt. 33:29

T

Teacher	Mark 9:17
Teacher, the	Matt. 26:18
Teacher who has come from God, a	John 3:2
Tower from the enemy, a strong	Ps. 61:3
Trust from my youth, my	Ps. 71:5
Truth, the	John 14:6

V

Vine, the	John 15:5
Vinedresser, the	John 15:1
Vine, the true	John 15:1
Voice of the almighty, the Shaddai	Ezek. 1:24
Voice of the Lord	Ps. 29:3

W

Worry, the	John 14:6
Wisdom from God	1 Cor. 1:30
Wisdom of God, the	1 Cor. 1:24

Witness to the people, a	Isa. 55:4
Witness, faithful and true	Rev. 3:14
Witness, my	Job 16:19
Witness, the faithful	Rev. 1:5
Word of God	Rev. 19:13
Word of life, the	1 John 1:1
Word, the logos	John 1:1

Y

You who dwell in the heavens	Ps. 123:1
You who hear prayer	Ps. 65:2
You who judge righteously, testing	Jer. 11:20

For more copies, write to

Antioch Faith Tabernacle
P.O. BOX 600113
N. Miami Beach, Fl. 33160
USA
Phone # 305-754-4996
info@afaithtab.com

ISBN. 0-9766642-0-8 52500

NOTES

E.M. Bounds. *The Weapons of Prayer.* Whitaker House

Hugh Latimer. *Fox's Book of Martyrs*

Frances Ridley, Havergal. *J. Vernon McGee's Thru The Bible*

Girolamo Savoranola *J. Vernon McGee's Thru The Bible*

Dr. Thomas Cranmer. *Foxe's Book of Christian Martyrs*

Dr. Cranmer. *Adam Clarke's Commentary*

Williams Carvosso *The Complete Works of E. M. Bounds* by Bridge Logos

Jonathan Edwards *The Complete Works of E. M. Bounds* by Bridge Logos

John Knox. *Barclay's Daily Study Bible* (NT)

John Knox. John Flavel. *Treasury of David, The*

Bishop Polycarp. *Adam Clarke's Commentary*

Dr Norman Walker. *Water Can Undermine Your Health?* (Prescott, AZ: Norwalk Press, 1974

Webster's Unabridged New Twentieth-Century Dictionary. World Publishing Company